The Pictor

Ar

Published: 1910
Categorie(s): Non-Fiction

About Waite:

Arthur Edward Waite while born in America, is better known as an English mystic, occultist and prolific writer on Masonic and esoteric subjects. A member of the famous occult order, the Hermetic Order of the Golden Dawn, Waite has had published a number of important books on esoteric matters. His most lasting legacy however, is not through his books, but via the Tarot deck he created. Called the Rider Waite Tarot Deck, it is perhaps the most popular tarot deck to have come out of the twentieth century.

Arthur Waite was born in Brooklyn, NY, on the 2nd of October 1857. His father Charles F. Waite was a Capt in the American Merchant Marine, while his mother Emma Lovell was the English daughter of a wealthy London merchant involved in the East India trade. Just a year after he was born and while on a voyage from Connecticut to London, Waite's father died at sea on the 29th September 1858. Widowed and pregnant at the time, after giving birth to his sister Frederika, Emma and the children returned to London, England.

What is not generally known, is that the children had been born illegitimately, for Emma and Capt Waite had never been legally married, her family had objected to it. On her return to London and due to her family's continued ostracism, she was forced to rear her children in the poorer less fashionable suburbs of north and west London. The rejection of her family also caused her to convert to the Roman Catholic Church, a faith she past on to her son and daughter.

While they were not very well off, Emma did her best to educated Waite, first at small private schools in North London, and then at St. Charles's College, a Roman Catholic school in Baywater. After leaving school, Waite started work as a clerk and in his spare time wrote poetry and romantic fiction. Waite spent much of his life in and around London, as a prolific writer he soon became connected with various publishing houses. His first published work was 'An Ode to Astronomy' (1877), after which he published many poems and stories in minor literary journals, later he also edited a small magazine The Unknown World. In 1886 his first major work on the occult appeared: 'The Mysteries of Magic, a Digest of the writings of Eliphas Levi' (Redway 1886).

After his sister's death in 1874, Waite lost interest in the Roman Catholic Church, but retained a great love for its ritual ceremony, in his later associations with secret Orders; he would utilize various aspects of Roman Catholicism in his own ritual constructions. Waite then began to explore alternate paths of spirituality and occultism. He started with Spiritualism, but found it not to his liking and moved on to the Theosophical Society. This he found fascinating, but disapproved of the anti-Christian bias he found in the works of H. P. Blavatsky, its leading driving force.

By this time Waite was a regularly reader at the Library of the British Museum, studying many branches of esotericism. It was here that he came across the writings and teachings of Eliphas Levi, and realized where his direction lay. While he had already written and published numerous poems and romances, he also recognized his shortcomings as a writer of fiction, and therefore decided to concentrate on a career as a critic and compiler on the history and doctrines of occultism. It was here while studying at the British Museum that he first came into contact with the likes of S.L. MacGregor Mathers, one of the original founders of the 'Order of the Golden Dawn', but at the time he didn't liked him.

In 1883/1884 he married Ada Lakeman 'Lucasta' with whom he had one daughter Sybil Waite. Later in January 1891, Waite and 'Lucasta' were initiated into the Neophyte grade of the Order of the Golden Dawn. The initiation took place at the Mathers' house, Stent Lodge in Dulwich, near to the Horniman Museum were Mathers worked. However, 'Lucasta' was never enthusiastic and Waite's attendance and involvement was sporadic. Waite had always been biased in favor of the path of the Mystic rather than that of the Occultist, so he didn't always see eye to eye with Mathers and never felt happy in the original Golden Dawn. However he persisted and by April 1892 had advanced to the $4 = 7$ grade of Philosophus.

Waite still not feeling happy in the order, left in 1893 only to return again in 1896 and continue working through the grades. In 1899 he entered the Second Order and began working his way to the top. However the Order had already started its downward slide, when in 1897 Dr. Westcott as the head of the order in London, was forced to resign and Florence Farr the famous stage actress took over. Still under the direction of Mathers in Paris, Farr's relationship with Mathers was strained and she lacked Dr. Westcott's practical management abilities. After his leaving, the extensive grade-work and examination system of the Second Order began to deteriorate and the whole London order slipped into decline.

In the meantime to aid his own progress, Waite turned his attention to Freemasonry. On the 19th September 1901, he was initiated into the Runymede Lodge No. 2430 at Wraysbury, Bucks, and raised on the 10th February 1902 in the St. Marylebone Lodge No. 1305. This was a good step for Waite to make for many influential people involved in the Grand Lodge who had previously resented his researches, were also high-level members of the Golden Dawn. Two months later in April 1902, he also joined The Societas Rosicruciana in Anglia (S.R.I.A.), which also contained leading members of the Golden Dawn.

After he had been raised, Waite began his quest for higher degrees in earnest, and proceeded to the Holy Royal Arch, being exalted in Metropolitan Chapter No. 1507 on 1 May 1902, following this a week later with his Installation as a Knights Templar at the Consecration of the King Edward VII Preceptory. Waite had formulated the theory that all esoteric practices and traditions, whether Alchemy, Hebrew Kabbalah, Legends of the Holy Grail, Rosicrucianism, Christian Mysticism or Freemasonry, were secret paths to a direct experience of God. He was convinced that the symbolism in each of these traditions had a common root and a common end, and that their correct interpretation would lead to a revelation of concealed ways to spiritual illumination.

In 1910 Waite was installed as the Master of Runymede Lodge, and while he pursued his other interests, he always remained a loyal member, contributed to its lectures and regularly attended its meetings. That is until 1920, when he moved from London to Ramsgate in Kent. By which time his association with Craft Masonry had faded, as he released his memberships with other fraternities, though he remained a member of his Mother Lodge until his death.

By 1903, the original Order of the Golden Dawn had been racked by feuds, schisms and scandals, and the order as it had been finally split up into separate and independent groups. Those who remained loyal to Mathers formed the "Order of the Alpha et Omega Temple", while Waite took over as head of the original Isis-Urania Temple. Many of the remaining Golden Dawn members stayed with Waite's group, which he renamed the Order of the Independent and Rectified Rite.

However many of the old group didn't like the new Order, for Waite did not care for magic and replaced it with mysticism. This led to another schism and the more magically inclined members including Dr. Robert William Felkin and John William Brodie-Innes, left to form the "Order of the Stella Matutina". The new Order struggled on for a few years but continued to be dogged by dissidents; further feuds followed until Waite dissolved the Order in 1914.

He replaced it the following year with the Fellowship of the Rosy Cross, making clear in its constitution it's independence from all other Orders. One clause stated that: "The Fellowship of the Rosy Cross has no concern whatsoever in occult or psychical research, it is a Quest of Grace and not a Quest of Power". Another clause stated: "The Independent and Rectified Rite with its dependencies, if any, in so far as now in activity, and the Stella Matutina Temple together with its dependencies, are not in communication with the Fellowship of the Rosy Cross, and cannot be Visited or Joined".

The Fellowship of the Rosy Cross as did many of the other factions created after the demise of the Golden Dawn, gradually lost its momentum and faded into history. After the demise of the Fellowship, it was rumored that his marriage to 'Lucasta' had deteriorated, and that he had taken up and was living with his secretary in Penywern Road, Earl's Court, London. She it turns out was an ex–member of the Isis-Urania Temple whose motto was Vigilate, which was most appropriate for other rumors circulated that he had taken to drink. She appears to have doted on him hand and foot, and helped him through a difficult time. In 1920, Waite moved from London to Ramsgate in Kent, there to concentrate on his writings. After the death of 'Lucasta's' in 1924, he married Mary Broadbent Schofield (Una Salus).

Waite died on the 19th of May 1943 and was buried in the churchyard at Bishopsbourne in Kent, where he spent most of his later years. Despite his prolific contributions to the rituals and lectures that make up the history of Freemasonry, he was accorded just a brief, three-paragraph obituary in The Freemasons' Chronicle (vol. 135, p. 178, 6 June 1942). In it he was merely characterized as a poet and writer on Freemasonry. Waite's grave is now obscured by a thick growth of deadly nightshade, an appropriate parallel to the blight that has fallen on his reputation.

A prolific writer of over seventy books, lectures, rituals and contributions to many journals and magazines, Waite's lasting legacy is not through his writing, but through his creation of the Rider Waite

Tarot Deck. In the early 1900's as head of the reconstructed Isis-Urania Temple of the Golden Dawn, Waite had just completed his book 'The Key to the Tarot' and needed someone to illustrate it. One of his members was an accomplished artist Pamela Colman Smith; he commissioned and directed her in the design of a beautiful set of cards. The main innovation being the illustration of all cards, not just the Major arcana but the Minor cards too, and in such a way as to be pictorially suggestive of their divinatory meanings. He also made popular the spread known as the Celtic Cross, which was then taught in the First Order of the Golden Dawn.

Of his writings and scholarly pursuits, Waite produced translations of Eliphas Levi and Papus, as well as re-issues of mystical and alchemical works such as those of Thomas Vaughan. Some of his main works include:

The Mysteries of Magic (1886)
Handbook of Cartomancy (1889)
The Occult Sciences (Keagan Paul – 1891)
Devil-Worship in France (Redway 1896)
Louis Claude de Saint-Martin (1901)
Studies in Mysticism (1906)
A New Encyclopaedia of Freemasonry (1921)
Emblematic Freemasonry (1925)
The Secret Tradition in Freemasonry (1937)
His autobiographical Shadows of Life and Thought (1938)

Other books include: Book of Ceremonial Magic, Book of the Holy Grail, Quest of the Golden Stairs, Belle and the Dragon, Unknown World, Works of Thomas Vaughan, The Way of Divine Union, Strange

Houses of Sleep, Azoth or the Star in the East, Book of Spells, Collected Poems of Arthur Edward Waite, The Golden Dawn Tarot, Hermetic and Alchemical Writings of Paracelsus, Hidden Church of the Holy Grail, Raymond Lully: Illuminated Doctor, Alchemist and Christian Mystic, Secret Doctrine in Israel, Three Famous Mystics, Turba Philosophorum, Understanding the Tarot Deck, and The Way of Divine Union.

Finally, during his life, Waite may well have developed from a poor background and poor education, into a snobbish man of distinction, contemptuous and critical of his contemporaries, he certainly ruffled a few feathers during his time. But isn't that the trait of many a great man? Despite dedicating much of his life to Freemasonry, few if any masons in England would seem to think so. Not so in America, were a large collection of his writings, lectures and letters, have been collected and stored for prosperity in the Iowa Grand Lodge Library, Ceder Rapids. USA.

Summary:

The book consists of three parts.

Part I, "The Veil and Its Symbols", is a short overview of the traditional symbols associated with each card, followed by a history of the Tarot. Waite dismissed as baseless the belief that the Tarot was Egyptian in origin, and noted that no evidence of the cards exists prior to the 15th century.

Part II, "The Doctrine of the Veil", contains 78 black and white plates of the Rider-Waite-Smith deck, and a discussion of the unique symbols chosen for each card. Waite drew upon the earlier Tarot of French occultist Eliphas Levi, at times retaining his changes to the traditional deck (as with the Chariot card, which both Waite and Levi picture being drawn by two sphinx, instead of horses), at other times criticizing him (as with the Hermit card, which Waite thought Levi misinterpreted).

Part III, "The Outer Methods of the Oracles", concerns matters of divination with the cards, including a description of the famous Celtic Cross Tarot layout, which the book helped popularize.

Preface

IT seems rather of necessity than predilection in the sense of apologia that I should put on record in the first place a plain statement of my personal position, as one who for many years of literary life has been, subject to his spiritual and other limitations, an exponent of the higher mystic schools. It will be thought that I am acting strangely in concerning myself at this day with what appears at first sight and simply a well-known method of fortune-telling. Now, the opinions of Mr. Smith, even in the literary reviews, are of no importance unless they happen to agree with our own, but in order to sanctify this doctrine we must take care that our opinions, and the subjects out of which they arise, are concerned only with the highest. Yet it is just this which may seem doubtful, in the present instance, not only to Mr. Smith, whom I respect within the proper measures of detachment, but to some of more real consequence, seeing that their dedications are mine. To these and to any I would say that after the most illuminated Frater Christian Rosy Cross had beheld the Chemical Marriage in the Secret Palace of Transmutation, his story breaks off abruptly, with an intimation that he expected next morning to be door-keeper. After the same manner, it happens more often than might seem likely that those who have seen the King of Heaven through the most clearest veils of the sacraments are those who assume thereafter the humblest offices of all about the House of God. By such simple devices also are the Adepts and Great Masters in the secret orders distinguished from the cohort of Neophytes as servi servorum mysterii. So also, or in a way which is not entirely unlike, we meet with the Tarot cards at the outermost gates—amidst the fritterings and debris of the so-called occult arts, about which no one in their senses has suffered the smallest deception; and yet these cards belong in themselves to another region, for they contain a very high symbolism, which is interpreted according to the Laws of Grace rather than by the pretexts and intuitions of that which passes for divination. The fact that the wisdom of God is foolishness with men does not create a presumption that the foolishness of this world makes in any sense for Divine Wisdom; so neither the scholars in the ordinary classes nor the pedagogues in the seats of the mighty will be quick to perceive the likelihood or even the possibility of this proposition. The subject has been in the hands of cartomancists as part of the stock-in-trade of their industry; I do not seek to persuade any one outside my own circles that this is of much or of no consequence; but on the historical and interpretative sides it has not fared better; it has been there in the hands of exponents who have brought it into utter contempt for those people who possess philosophical insight or faculties for the appreciation of evidence. It is time that it should be rescued, and this I propose to undertake once and for all, that I may have done with the side issues which distract from the term. As poetry is the most beautiful expression of the things that are of all most beautiful, so is symbolism the most catholic expression in concealment of things that are most profound in the Sanctuary and that have not been declared outside it with the same fulness by means of the spoken word. The justification of the rule of silence is no part of my present concern, but I have put on record elsewhere, and quite recently, what it is possible to say on this subject.

The little treatise which follows is divided into three parts, in the first of which I have dealt with the antiquities of the subject and a few things that arise from and connect therewith. It should be understood that it is not put forward as a contribution to the history of playing cards, about which I know and care nothing; it is a consideration dedicated and addressed to a certain school of occultism, more especially in France, as to the source and centre of all the phantasmagoria which has entered into expression during the last fifty years under the pretence of considering Tarot cards historically. In the second part, I have dealt with the symbolism according to some of its higher aspects, and this also serves to introduce the complete and rectified Tarot, which is available separately, in the form of coloured cards, the designs of which are added to the present text in black and white. They have been prepared under my supervision—in respect of the attributions and meanings—by a lady who has high claims as an artist. Regarding the divinatory part, by which my thesis is terminated, I consider it personally as a fact in the history of the Tarot—as such, I have drawn, from all published sources, a harmony of the meanings which have been attached to the various cards, and I have given prominence to one method of working that has not been published previously; having the merit of simplicity, while it is also of universal application, it may be held to replace the cumbrous and involved systems of the larger hand-books.

Part 1
The Veil And Its Symbols

Introductory and General

THE pathology of the poet says that "the undevout astronomer is mad"; the pathology of the very plain man says that genius is mad; and between these extremes, which stand for ten thousand analogous excesses, the sovereign reason takes the part of a moderator and does what it can. I do not think that there is a pathology of the occult dedications, but about their extravagances no one can question, and it is not less difficult than thankless to act as a moderator regarding them. Moreover, the pathology, if it existed, would probably be an empiricism rather than a diagnosis, and would offer no criterion. Now, occultism is not like mystic faculty, and it very seldom works in harmony either with business aptitude in the things of ordinary life or with a knowledge of the canons of evidence in its own sphere. I know that for the high art of ribaldry there are few things more dull than the criticism which maintains that a thesis is untrue, and cannot understand that it is decorative. I know also that after long dealing with doubtful doctrine or with difficult research it is always refreshing, in the domain of this art, to meet with what is obviously of fraud or at least of complete unreason. But the aspects of history, as seen through the lens of occultism, are not as a rule decorative, and have few gifts of refreshment to heal the lacerations which they inflict on the logical understanding. It almost requires a Frater Sapiens dominabitur astris in the Fellowship of the Rosy Cross to have the patience which is not lost amidst clouds of folly when the consideration of the Tarot is undertaken in accordance with the higher law of symbolism. The true Tarot is symbolism; it speaks no other language and offers no other signs. Given the inward meaning of its emblems, they do become a kind of alphabet which is capable of indefinite combinations and makes true sense in all. On the highest plane it offers a key to the Mysteries, in a manner which is not arbitrary and has not been read in, But the wrong symbolical stories have been told concerning it, and the wrong history has been given in every published work which so far has dealt with the subject. It has been intimated by two or three writers that, at least in respect of the meanings, this is unavoidably the case, because few are acquainted with them, while these few hold by transmission under pledges and cannot betray their trust. The suggestion is fantastic on the surface for there seems a certain anti-climax in the proposition that a particular interpretation of fortune-telling—l'art de tirer les cartes—can be reserved for Sons of the Doctrine. The fact remains, notwithstanding, that a Secret Tradition exists regarding the Tarot, and as there is always the possibility that some minor arcana of the Mysteries may be made public with a flourish of trumpets, it will be as well to go before the event and to warn those who are curious in such matters that any revelation will contain only a third part of the earth and sea and a third part of the stars of heaven in respect of the symbolism. This is for the simple reason that neither in root-matter nor in development has more been put into writing, so that much will remain to be said after any pretended unveiling. The guardians of certain temples of initiation who keep watch over mysteries of this order have therefore no cause for alarm.

In my preface to The Tarot of the Bohemians, which, rather by an accident of things, has recently come to be re-issued after a long period, I have said what was then possible or seemed most necessary. The present work is designed more especially—as I have intimated—to introduce a rectified set of the cards themselves and to tell the unadorned truth concerning them, so far as this is possible in the outer circles. As regards the sequence of greater symbols, their ultimate and highest meaning lies deeper than the common language of picture or hieroglyph. This will be understood by those who have received some part of the Secret Tradition. As regards the verbal meanings allocated here to the more important Trump Cards, they are designed to set aside the follies and impostures of past attributions, to put those who have the gift of insight on the right track, and to take care, within the limits of my possibilities, that they are the truth so far as they go.

It is regrettable in several respects that I must confess to certain reservations, but there is a question of honour at issue. Furthermore, between the follies on the one side of those who know nothing of the tradition, yet are in their own opinion the exponents of something called occult science and philosophy, and on the other side between the make-believe of a few writers who have received part of the tradition and think that it constitutes a legal title to scatter dust in the eyes of the world without, I feel that the time has come to say what it is possible to say, so that the effect of current charlatanism and unintelligence may be reduced to a minimum.

We shall see in due course that the history of Tarot cards is largely of a negative kind, and that, when the issues are cleared by the dissipation of reveries and gratuitous speculations expressed in the terms of certitude, there is in fact no history prior to the fourteenth century. The deception and self-deception regarding their origin in Egypt, India or China put a lying spirit into the mouths of the first expositors, and the later occult writers have done little more than reproduce the first false testimony in the good faith of an intelligence unawakened to the issues of research. As it so happens, all expositions have worked within a very narrow range, and owe, comparatively speaking, little to the inventive faculty. One brilliant opportunity has at least been missed, for it has not so far occurred to any one that the Tarot might perhaps have done duty and even originated as a secret symbolical language of the Albigensian sects. I commend this suggestion to the lineal descendants in the spirit of Gabriele Rossetti and Eugene Aroux, to Mr. Harold Bayley as another New Light on the Renaissance, and as a taper at least in the darkness which, with great respect, might be serviceable to the zealous and all-searching mind of Mrs. Cooper-Oakley. Think only what the supposed testimony of watermarks on paper might gain from the Tarot card of the Pope or Hierophant, in connexion with the notion of a secret Albigensian patriarch, of which Mr. Bayley has found in these same watermarks so much material to his purpose. Think only for a moment about the card of the High Priestess as representing the Albigensian church itself; and think of the Tower struck by Lightning as typifying the desired destruction of Papal Rome, the city on the seven hills, with the pontiff and his temporal power cast down from the spiritual edifice when it is riven by the wrath of God. The possibilities are so numerous and persuasive that they almost deceive in their expression one of the elect who has invented them. But there is more even than this, though I scarcely dare to cite it. When the time came for the Tarot cards to be the subject of their first formal explanation, the archaeologist Court de Gebelin reproduced some of their most important emblems, and—if I may so term it—the codex which he used has served—by means of his engraved plates-as a basis of reference for many sets that have been issued subsequently. The figures are very primitive and differ as such from the cards of Etteilla, the Marseilles Tarot, and others still current in France. I am not a good judge in such matters, but the fact that every one of the Trumps Major might have answered for watermark purposes is shewn by the cases which I have quoted and by one most remarkable example of the Ace of Cups.

I should call it an eucharistic emblem after the manner of a ciborium, but this does not signify at the moment. The point is that Mr. Harold Bayley gives six analogous devices in his New Light on the Renaissance, being watermarks on paper of the seventeenth century, which he claims to be of Albigensian origin and to represent sacramental and Graal emblems. Had he only heard of the Tarot, had he known that these cards of

divination, cards of fortune, cards of all vagrant arts, were perhaps current at the period in the South of France, I think that his enchanting but all too fantastic hypothesis might have dilated still more largely in the atmosphere of his dream. We should no doubt have had a vision of Christian Gnosticism, Manichaeanism, and all that he understands by pure primitive Gospel, shining behind the pictures.

I do not look through such glasses, and I can only commend the subject to his attention at a later period; it is mentioned here that I may introduce with an unheard-of wonder the marvels of arbitrary speculation as to the history of the cards.

With reference to their form and number, it should scarcely be necessary to enumerate them, for they must be almost commonly familiar, but as it is precarious to assume anything, and as there are also other reasons, I will tabulate them briefly as follows:—

The Trumps Major, otherwise Greater Arcana

1. The Magus, Magician, or juggler, the caster of the dice and mountebank, in the world of vulgar trickery. This is the colportage interpretation, and it has the same correspondence with the real symbolical meaning that the use of the Tarot in fortune-telling has with its mystic construction according to the secret science of symbolism. I should add that many independent students of the subject, following their own lights, have produced individual sequences of meaning in respect of the Trumps Major, and their lights are sometimes suggestive, but they are not the true lights. For example, Eliphas Levi says that the Magus signifies that unity which is the mother of numbers; others say that it is the Divine Unity; and one of the latest French commentators considers that in its general sense it is the will.

2. The High Priestess, the Pope Joan, or Female Pontiff; early expositors have sought to term this card the Mother, or Pope's Wife, which is opposed to the symbolism. It is sometimes held to represent the Divine Law and the Gnosis, in which case the Priestess corresponds to the idea of the Shekinah. She is the Secret Tradition and the higher sense of the instituted Mysteries.

3. The Empress, who is sometimes represented with full face, while her correspondence, the Emperor, is in profile. As there has been some tendency to ascribe a symbolical significance to this distinction, it seems desirable to say that it carries no inner meaning. The

Empress has been connected with the ideas of universal fecundity and in a general sense with activity.

4. The Emperor, by imputation the spouse of the former. He is occasionally represented as wearing, in addition to his personal insignia, the stars or ribbons of some order of chivalry. I mention this to shew that the cards are a medley of old and new emblems. Those who insist upon the evidence of the one may deal, if they can, with the other. No effectual argument for the antiquity of a particular design can be drawn from the fact that it incorporates old material; but there is also none which can be based on sporadic novelties, the intervention of which may signify only the unintelligent hand of an editor or of a late draughtsman.

5. The High Priest or Hierophant, called also Spiritual Father, and more commonly and obviously the Pope. It seems even to have been named the Abbot, and then its correspondence, the High Priestess, was the Abbess or Mother of the Convent. Both are arbitrary names. The insignia of the figures are papal, and in such case the High Priestess is and can be only the Church, to whom Pope and priests are married by the spiritual rite of ordination. I think, however, that in its primitive form this card did not represent the Roman Pontiff.

6. The Lovers or Marriage. This symbol has undergone many variations, as might be expected from its subject. In the eighteenth century form, by which it first became known to the world of archaeological research, it is really a card of married life, shewing father and mother, with their child placed between them; and the pagan Cupid above, in the act of flying his shaft, is, of course, a misapplied emblem. The Cupid is of love beginning rather than of love in its fulness, guarding the

fruit thereof. The card is said to have been entitled Simulacyum fidei, the symbol of conjugal faith, for which the rainbow as a sign of the covenant would have been a more appropriate concomitant. The figures are also held to have signified Truth, Honour and Love, but I suspect that this was, so to speak, the gloss of a commentator moralizing. It has these, but it has other and higher aspects.

7. The Chariot. This is represented in some extant codices as being drawn by two sphinxes, and the device is in consonance with the symbolism, but it must not be supposed that such was its original form; the variation was invented to support a particular historical hypothesis. In the eighteenth century white horses were yoked to the car. As regards its usual name, the lesser stands for the greater; it is really the King in his triumph, typifying, however, the victory which creates kingship as its natural consequence and not the vested royalty of the fourth card. M. Court de Gebelin said that it was Osiris Triumphing, the conquering sun in springtime having vanquished the obstacles of winter. We know now that Osiris rising from the dead is not represented by such obvious symbolism. Other animals than horses have also been used to draw the currus triumphalis, as, for example, a lion and a leopard.

8. Fortitude. This is one of the cardinal virtues, of which I shall speak later. The female figure is usually represented as closing the mouth of a lion. In the earlier form which is printed by Court de Gebelin, she is obviously opening it. The first alternative is better symbolically, but either is an instance of strength in its conventional understanding, and conveys the idea of mastery. It has been said that the figure represents organic force, moral force and the principle of all force.

9. The Hermit, as he is termed in common parlance, stands next on the list; he is also the Capuchin, and in more philosophical language the Sage. He is said to be in search of that Truth which is located far off in the sequence, and of justice which has preceded him on the way. But this is a card of attainment, as we shall see later, rather than a card of quest. It is said also that his lantern contains the Light of Occult Science and that his staff is a Magic Wand. These interpretations are comparable in every respect to the divinatory and fortune-telling meanings with which I shall have to deal in their turn. The diabolism of both is that they are true after their own manner, but that they miss all the high things to which the Greater Arcana should be allocated. It is as if a man who knows in his heart that all roads lead to the heights, and that God is at the great height of all, should choose the way of perdition or the way of folly as the path of his own attainment. Eliphas Levi has allocated this card to Prudence, but in so doing he has been actuated by the wish to fill a gap which would otherwise occur in the symbolism. The four cardinal virtues are necessary to an idealogical sequence like the Trumps Major, but they must not be taken only in that first sense which exists for the use and consolation of him who in these days of halfpenny journalism is called the man in the street. In their proper understanding they are the correlatives of the counsels of perfection when these have been similarly re-expressed, and they read as follows: (a) Transcendental justice, the counter-equilibrium of the scales, when they have been overweighted so that they dip heavily on the side of God. The corresponding counsel is to use loaded dice when you play for high stakes with Diabolus. The axiom is Aut Deus, aut nihil. (b) Divine Ecstacy, as a counterpoise to something called Temperance, the sign

of which is, I believe, the extinction of lights in the tavern. The corresponding counsel is to drink only of new wine in the Kingdom of the Father, because God is all in all. The axiom is that man being a reasonable being must get intoxicated with God; the imputed case in point is Spinoza. (c) The state of Royal Fortitude, which is the state of a Tower of Ivory and a House of Gold, but it is God and not the man who has become Turris fortitudinis a facie inimici, and out of that House the enemy has been cast. The corresponding counsel is that a man must not spare himself even in the presence of death, but he must be certain that his sacrifice shall be-of any open course-the best that will ensure his end. The axiom is that the strength which is raised to such a degree that a man dares lose himself shall shew him how God is found, and as to such refuge—dare therefore and learn. (d) Prudence is the economy which follows the line of least resistance, that the soul may get back whence it came. It is a doctrine of divine parsimony and conservation of energy, because of the stress, the terror and the manifest impertinences of this life. The corresponding counsel is that true prudence is concerned with the one thing needful, and the axiom is: Waste not, want not. The conclusion of the whole matter is a business proposition founded on the law of exchange: You cannot help getting what you seek in respect of the things that are Divine: it is the law of supply and demand. I have mentioned these few matters at this point for two simple reasons: (a) because in proportion to the impartiality of the mind it seems sometimes more difficult to determine whether it is vice or vulgarity which lays waste the present world more piteously; (b) because in order to remedy the imperfections of the old notions it is highly needful, on occasion, to empty terms and phrases of their accepted significance, that they may receive a new and more adequate meaning.

10. The Wheel of Fortune. There is a current Manual of Cartomancy which has obtained a considerable vogue in England, and amidst a great scattermeal of curious things to no purpose has intersected a few serious subjects. In its last and largest edition it treats in one section of the Tarot; which—if I interpret the author rightly—it regards from beginning to end as the Wheel of Fortune, this expression being understood in my own sense. I have no objection to such an inclusive though conventional description; it obtains in all the worlds, and I wonder that it has not been adopted previously as the most appropriate name on the side of common fortune-telling. It is also the title of one of the Trumps Major—that indeed of our concern at the moment, as my sub-title shews. Of recent years this has suffered many fantastic presentations and one hypothetical reconstruction which is suggestive in its symbolism. The wheel has seven radii; in the eighteenth century the ascending and descending animals were really of nondescript character, one of them having a human head. At the summit was another monster with the body of an indeterminate beast, wings on shoulders and a crown on head. It carried two wands in its claws. These are replaced in the reconstruction by a Hermanubis rising with the wheel, a Sphinx couchant at the summit and a Typhon on the descending side. Here is another instance of an invention in support of a hypothesis; but if the latter be set aside the grouping is symbolically correct and can pass as such.

11. Justice. That the Tarot, though it is of all reasonable antiquity, is not of time immemorial, is shewn by this card, which could have been presented in a much more archaic manner. Those, however, who have gifts of discernment in matters of this kind will not

need to be told that age is in no sense of the essence of the consideration; the Rite of Closing the Lodge in the Third Craft Grade of Masonry may belong to the late eighteenth century, but the fact signifies nothing; it is still the summary of all the instituted and official Mysteries. The female figure of the eleventh card is said to be Astraea, who personified the same virtue and is represented by the same symbols. This goddess notwithstanding, and notwithstanding the vulgarian Cupid, the Tarot is not of Roman mythology, or of Greek either. Its presentation of justice is supposed to be one of the four cardinal virtues included in the sequence of Greater Arcana; but, as it so happens, the fourth emblem is wanting, and it became necessary for the commentators to discover it at all costs. They did what it was possible to do, and yet the laws of research have never succeeded in extricating the missing Persephone under the form of Prudence. Court de Gebelin attempted to solve the difficulty by a tour de force, and believed that he had extracted what he wanted from the symbol of the Hanged Man—wherein he deceived himself. The Tarot has, therefore, its justice, its Temperance also and its Fortitude, but—owing to a curious omission—it does not offer us any type of Prudence, though it may be admitted that, in some respects, the isolation of the Hermit, pursuing a solitary path by the light of his own lamp, gives, to those who can receive it, a certain high counsel in respect of the via prudentiae.

12. The Hanged Man. This is the symbol which is supposed to represent Prudence, and Eliphas Levi says, in his most shallow and plausible manner, that it is the adept bound by his engagements. The figure of a man is suspended head-downwards from a gibbet, to which he is attached by a rope about one of his ankles. The arms are bound behind him, and one leg is crossed over the

other. According to another, and indeed the prevailing interpretation, he signifies sacrifice, but all current meanings attributed to this card are cartomancists' intuitions, apart from any real value on the symbolical side. The fortune-tellers of the eighteenth century who circulated Tarots, depict a semi-feminine youth in jerkin, poised erect on one foot and loosely attached to a short stake driven into the ground.

13. Death. The method of presentation is almost invariable, and embodies a bourgeois form of symbolism. The scene is the field of life, and amidst ordinary rank vegetation there are living arms and heads protruding from the ground. One of the heads is crowned, and a skeleton with a great scythe is in the act of mowing it. The transparent and unescapable meaning is death, but the alternatives allocated to the symbol are change and transformation. Other heads have been swept from their place previously, but it is, in its current and patent meaning, more especially a card of the death of Kings. In the exotic sense it has been said to signify the ascent of the spirit in the divine spheres, creation and destruction, perpetual movement, and so forth.

14. Temperance. The winged figure of a female—who, in opposition to all doctrine concerning the hierarchy of angels, is usually allocated to this order of ministering spirits—is pouring liquid from one pitcher to another. In his last work on the Tarot, Dr. Papus abandons the traditional form and depicts a woman wearing an Egyptian head-dress. The first thing which seems clear on the surface is that the entire symbol has no especial connexion with Temperance, and the fact that this designation has always obtained for the card offers a very obvious instance of a meaning behind

meaning, which is the title in chief to consideration in respect of the Tarot as a whole.

15. The Devil. In the eighteenth century this card seems to have been rather a symbol of merely animal impudicity. Except for a fantastic head-dress, the chief figure is entirely naked; it has bat-like wings, and the hands and feet are represented by the claws of a bird. In the right hand there is a sceptre terminating in a sign which has been thought to represent fire. The figure as a whole is not particularly evil; it has no tail, and the commentators who have said that the claws are those of a harpy have spoken at random. There is no better ground for the alternative suggestion that they are eagle's claws. Attached, by a cord depending from their collars, to the pedestal on which the figure is mounted, are two small demons, presumably male and female. These are tailed, but not winged. Since 1856 the influence of Eliphas Levi and his doctrine of occultism has changed the face of this card, and it now appears as a pseudo-Baphometic figure with the head of a goat and a great torch between the horns; it is seated instead of erect, and in place of the generative organs there is the Hermetic caduceus. In Le Tarot Divinatoire of Papus the small demons are replaced by naked human beings, male and female ' who are yoked only to each other. The author may be felicitated on this improved symbolism.

16. The Tower struck by Lightning. Its alternative titles are: Castle of Plutus, God's House and the Tower of Babel. In the last case, the figures falling therefrom are held to be Nimrod and his minister. It is assuredly a card of confusion, and the design corresponds, broadly speaking, to any of the designations except Maison Dieu, unless we are to understand that the House of God has been abandoned and the veil of the temple rent. It is

a little surprising that the device has not so far been allocated to the destruction Of Solomon's Temple, when the lightning would symbolize the fire and sword with which that edifice was visited by the King of the Chaldees.

17. The Star, Dog-Star, or Sirius, also called fantastically the Star of the Magi. Grouped about it are seven minor luminaries, and beneath it is a naked female figure, with her left knee upon the earth and her right foot upon the water. She is in the act of pouring fluids from two vessels. A bird is perched on a tree near her; for this a butterfly on a rose has been substituted in some later cards. So also the Star has been called that of Hope. This is one of the cards which Court de Gebelin describes as wholly Egyptian-that is to say, in his own reverie.

18. The Moon. Some eighteenth-century cards shew the luminary on its waning side; in the debased edition of Etteilla, it is the moon at night in her plenitude, set in a heaven of stars; of recent years the moon is shewn on the side of her increase. In nearly all presentations she is shining brightly and shedding the moisture of fertilizing dew in great drops. Beneath there are two towers, between which a path winds to the verge of the horizon. Two dogs, or alternatively a wolf and dog, are baying at the moon, and in the foreground there is water, through which a crayfish moves towards the land.

19. The Sun. The luminary is distinguished in older cards by chief rays that are waved and salient alternately and by secondary salient rays. It appears to shed its influence on earth not only by light and heat, but—like the moon—by drops of dew. Court de Gebelin termed these tears of gold and of pearl, just as he identified the

lunar dew with the tears of Isis. Beneath the dog-star there is a wall suggesting an enclosure-as it might be, a walled garden-wherein are two children, either naked or lightly clothed, facing a water, and gambolling, or running hand in hand. Eliphas Levi says that these are sometimes replaced by a spinner unwinding destinies, and otherwise by a much better symbol-a naked child mounted on a white horse and displaying a scarlet standard.

20. The Last judgment. I have spoken of this symbol already, the form of which is essentially invariable, even in the Etteilla set. An angel sounds his trumpet per sepulchra regionum, and the dead arise. It matters little that Etteilla omits the angel, or that Dr. Papus substitutes a ridiculous figure, which is, however, in consonance with the general motive of that Tarot set which accompanies his latest work. Before rejecting the transparent interpretation of the symbolism which is conveyed by the name of the card and by the picture which it presents to the eye, we should feel very sure of our ground. On the surface, at least, it is and can be only the resurrection of that triad—father, mother, child-whom we have met with already in the eighth card. M. Bourgeat hazards the suggestion that esoterically it is the symbol of evolution—of which it carries none of the signs. Others say that it signifies renewal, which is obvious enough; that it is the triad of human life; that it is the "generative force of the earth... and eternal life." Court de Gebelin makes himself impossible as usual, and points out that if the grave-stones were removed it could be accepted as a symbol of creation.

21—which, however, in most of the arrangements is the cipher card, number nothing—The Fool, Mate, or Unwise Man. Court de Gebelin places it at the head of the whole series as the zero or negative which is presupposed by numeration, and as this is a simpler so also it is a better arrangement. It has been abandoned because in later times the cards have been attributed to the letters of the Hebrew alphabet, and there has been apparently some difficulty about allocating the zero symbol satisfactorily in a sequence of letters all of which signify numbers. In the present reference of the card to the letter Shin, which corresponds to 200, the difficulty or the unreason remains. The truth is that the real arrangement of the cards has never transpired. The Fool carries a wallet; he is looking over his shoulder and does not know that he is on the brink of a precipice; but a dog or other animal—some call it a tiger—is attacking him from behind, and he is hurried to his destruction unawares. Etteilla has given a justifiable variation of this card—as generally understood—in the form of a court jester, with cap, bells and motley garb. The other descriptions say that the wallet contains the bearer's follies and vices, which seems bourgeois and arbitrary.

22. The World, the Universe, or Time. The four living creatures of the Apocalypse and Ezekiel's vision, attributed to the evangelists in Christian symbolism, are grouped about an elliptic garland, as if it were a chain of flowers intended to symbolize all sensible things; within this garland there is the figure of a woman, whom the wind has girt about the loins with a light scarf, and this is all her vesture. She is in the act of dancing, and has a wand in either hand. It is eloquent as an image of the swirl of the sensitive life, of joy attained in the body, of the soul's intoxication in the earthly paradise, but still guarded by the Divine Watchers, as if by the powers and the graces of the Holy Name, Tetragammaton, JVHV—those four ineffable letters which are sometimes attributed to the mystical beasts. Eliphas Levi calls the

garland a crown, and reports that the figure represents Truth. Dr. Papus connects it with the Absolute and the realization of the Great Work; for yet others it is a symbol of humanity and the eternal reward of a life that has been spent well. It should be noted that in the four quarters of the garland there are four flowers distinctively marked. According to P. Christian, the garland should be formed of roses, and this is the kind of chain which Eliphas Levi says is less easily broken than a chain of iron. Perhaps by antithesis, but for the same reason, the iron crown of Peter may he more lightly on the heads of sovereign pontiffs than the crown of gold on kings.

The Four Suits, otherwise Lesser Arcana

The resources of interpretation have been lavished, if not exhausted, on the twenty-two Trumps Major, the symbolism of which is unquestionable. There remain the four suits, being Wands or Sceptres—ex hypothesi, in the archaeology of the subject, the antecedents of Diamonds in modern cards: Cups, corresponding to Hearts; Swords, which answer to Clubs, as the weapon of chivalry is in relation to the peasant's quarter-staff or the Alsatian bludgeon; and, finally, Pentacles—called also Deniers and Money—which are the prototypes of Spades, In the old as in the new suits, there are ten numbered cards, but in the Tarot there are four Court Cards allocated to each suit, or a Knight in addition to King, Queen and Knave. The Knave is a page, valet, or damoiseau; most correctly, he is an esquire, presumably in the service of the Knight; but there are certain rare sets in which the page becomes a maid of honour, thus pairing the sexes in the tetrad of the court cards. There are naturally distinctive features in respect of the several pictures, by which I mean that the King of Wands is not exactly the same personage as the King of Cups, even after allowance has been made for the different emblems that they bear; but the symbolism resides in their rank and in the suit to which they belong. So also the smaller cards, which—until now—have never been issued pictorially in these our modem days, depend on the particular meaning attaching to their numbers in connexion with the particular suit. I reserve, therefore, the details of the Lesser Arcana, till I come to speak in the second part of the rectified and perfected Tarot which accompanies this work. The consensus of divinatory meanings attached both to the greater and lesser symbols belongs to the third part.

The Tarot in History

Our immediate next concern is to speak of the cards in their history, so that the speculations and reveries which have been perpetuated and multiplied in the schools of occult research may be disposed of once and for all, as intimated in the preface hereto.

Let it be understood at the beginning of this point that there are several sets or sequences of ancient cards which are only in part of our concern. The Tarot of the Bohemians, by Papus, which I have recently carried through the press, revising the imperfect rendering, has some useful information in this connexion, and, except for the omission of dates and other evidences of the archaeological sense, it will serve the purpose of the general reader. I do not propose to extend it in the present place in any manner that can be called considerable, but certain additions are desirable and so also is a distinct mode of presentation.

Among ancient cards which are mentioned in connexion with the Tarot, there are firstly those of Baldini, which are the celebrated set attributed by tradition to Andrea Mantegna, though this view is now generally rejected. Their date is supposed to be about 1470, and it is thought that there are not more than four collections extant in Europe. A copy or reproduction referred to 1485 is perhaps equally rare. A complete set contains fifty numbers, divided into five denaries or sequences of ten cards each. There seems to be no record that they were used for the purposes of a game, whether of chance or skill; they could scarcely have lent themselves to divination or any form of fortune-telling; while it would be more than idle to impute a profound symbolical meaning to their obvious emblematic designs. The first denary embodies Conditions of Life, as follows: (i) The Beggar, (2) the Knave, (3) the

Artisan, (4) the Merchant, (5) the Noble, (6) the Knight, (7) the Doge, (8) the King, (9) the Emperor, (10) the Pope. The second contains the Muses and their Divine Leader: (11) Calliope, (12) Urania, (13) Terpsichore, (14) Erato, (15) Polyhymnia, (16) Thalia, (17) Melpomene, (18) Euterpe, (19) Clio, (20) Apollo. The third combines part of the Liberal Arts and Sciences with other departments of human learning, as follows: (21) Grammar, (22) Logic, (23) Rhetoric, (24) Geometry, (25) Arithmetic, (26) Music, (27) Poetry,(28) Philosophy, (29) Astrology, (30) Theology. The fourth denary completes the Liberal Arts and enumerates the Virtues: (31) Astronomy, (32) Chronology, (33) Cosmology, (34) Temperance, (35) Prudence, (36) Strength, (37) Justice; (38) Charity, (39) Hope, (40) Faith. The fifth and last denary presents the System of the Heavens (41) Moon, (42) Mercury, (43) Venus, (44) Sun, (45) Mars, (46) Jupiter, (47) Saturn, (48) A Eighth Sphere, (49) Primum Mobile, (50) First Cause.

We mnst set aside the fantastic attempts to extract complete Tarot sequences out of these denaries; we must forbear from saying, for example, that the Conditions of Life correspond to the Trumps Major, the Muses to Pentacles, the Arts and Sciences to Cups, the Virtues, etc., to Sceptres, and the conditions of life to Swords. This kind of thing can be done by a process of mental contortion, but it has no place in reality. At the same time, it is hardly possible that individual cards should not exhibit certain, and even striking, analogies. The Baldini King, Knight and Knave suggest the corresponding court cards of the Minor Arcana. The Emperor, Pope, Temperance, Strength, justice, Moon and Sun are common to the Mantegna and Trumps Major of any Tarot pack. Predisposition has also connected the Beggar and Fool, Venus and the Star, Mars and the Chariot, Saturn and the Hermit, even

Jupiter, or alternatively the First Cause, with the Tarot card of the World.[1] But the most salient features of the Trumps Major are wanting in the Mantegna set, and I do not believe that the ordered sequence in the latter case gave birth, as it has been suggested, to the others. Romain Merlin maintained this view, and positively assigned the Baldini cards to the end of the fourteenth century.

[1. The beggar is practically naked, and the analogy is constituted by the presence of two dogs, one of which seems to be flying at his legs. The Mars card depicts a sword-bearing warrior in a canopied chariot, to which, however, no horses are attached. Of course, if the Baldini cards belong to the close of the fifteenth century, there is no question at issue, as the Tarot was known in Europe long before that period.]

If it be agreed that, except accidentally and sporadically, the Baldini emblematic or allegorical pictures have only a shadowy and occasional connexion with Tarot cards, and, whatever their most probable date, that they can have supplied no originating motive, it follows that we are still seeking not only an origin in place and time for the symbols with which we are concerned, but a specific case of their manifestation on the continent of Europe to serve as a point of departure, whether backward or forward. Now it is well known that in the year 1393 the painter Charles Gringonneur—who for no reason that I can trace has been termed an occultist and kabalist by one indifferent English writer—designed and illuminated some kind of cards for the diversion of Charles VI of France when he was in mental ill-health, and the question arises whether anything can be ascertained of their nature. The only available answer is that at Paris, in the Bibliotheque du Roi, there are seventeen cards drawn and illuminated on paper. They are very beautiful, antique and priceless; the figures have a background of gold, and are framed in a silver border; but they are accompanied by no inscription and no number.

It is certain, however, that they include Tarot Trumps Major, the list of which is as follows: Fool, Emperor, Pope, Lovers, Wheel of Fortune, Temperance, Fortitude, justice, Moon, Sun, Chariot, Hermit, Hanged Man, Death, Tower and Last judgment. There are also four Tarot Cards at the Musee Carrer, Venice, and five others elsewhere, making nine in all. They include two pages or Knaves, three Kings and two Queens, thus illustrating the Minor Arcana. These collections have all been identified with the set produced by Gringonneur, but the ascription was disputed so far back as the year 1848, and it is not apparently put forward at the present day, even by those who are anxious to make evident the antiquity of the Tarot. It is held that they are all of Italian and some at least certainly of Venetian origin. We have in this manner our requisite point of departure in respect of place at least. It has further been stated with authority that Venetian Tarots are the old and true form, which is the parent of all others; but I infer that complete sets of the Major and Minor Arcana belong to much later periods. The pack is thought to have consisted of seventy-eight cards.

Notwithstanding, however, the preference shewn towards the Venetian Tarot, it is acknowledged that some portions of a Minchiate or Florentine set must be allocated to the period between 1413 and 1418. These were once in the possession of Countess Gonzaga, at Milan. A complete Minchiate pack contained ninety-seven cards, and in spite of these vestiges it is regarded, speaking generally, as a later development. There were forty-one Trumps Major, the additional numbers being borrowed or reflected from the Baldini emblematic set. In the court cards of the Minor Arcana, the Knights were monsters of the centaur type, while the Knaves were sometimes warriors and sometimes serving-men. Another distinction dwelt upon is the prevalence of Chrstian mediaeval ideas and the utter absence of any Oriental suggestion. The question, however, remains whether there are Eastern traces in any Tarot cards.

We come, in fine, to the Bolognese Tarot, sometimes referred to as that of Venice and having the Trumps Major complete, but numbers 20 and 21 are transposed. In the Minor Arcana the 2, 3, 4 and 5 of the small cards are omitted, with the result that there are sixty-two cards in all. The termination of the Trumps Major in the representation of the Last judgment is curious, and a little arresting as a point of symbolism; but this is all that it seems necessary to remark about the pack of Bologna, except that it is said to have been invented—or, as a Tarot, more correctly, modified—about the beginning of the fifteenth century by an exiled Prince of Pisa resident in the city. The purpose for which they were used is made tolerably evident by the fact that, in 1423, St. Bernardin of Sienna preached against playing cards and other forms of gambling. Forty years later the importation of cards into England was forbidden, the time being that of King Edward IV. This is the first certain record of the subject in our country.

It is difficult to consult perfect examples of the sets enumerated above, but it is not difficult to meet with detailed and illustrated descriptions—I should add, provided always that the writer is not an occultist, for accounts emanating from that source are usually imperfect, vague and preoccupied by considerations which cloud the critical issues. An instance in point is offered by certain views which have been expressed on the Mantegna codex—if I may continue to dignify card sequences with a title of this kind. It has been ruled—as we have seen—in occult reverie that Apollo and the

Nine Muses are in correspondence with Pentacles, but the analogy does not obtain in a working state of research; and reverie must border on nightmare before we can identify Astronomy, Chronology and Cosmology with the suit of Cups. The Baldini figures which represent these subjects are emblems of their period and not symbols, like the Tarot.

In conclusion as to this part, I observe that there has been a disposition among experts to think that the Trumps Major were not originally connected with the numbered suits. I do not wish to offer a personal view; I am not an expert in the history of games of chance, and I hate the profanum vulgus of divinatory devices; but I venture, under all reserves, to intimate that if later research should justify such a leaning, then—except for the good old art of fortune-telling and its tamperings with so-called destiny—it will be so much the better for the Greater Arcana.

So far as regards what is indispensable as preliminaries to the historical aspects of Tarot cards, and I will now take up the speculative side of the subject and produce its tests of value. In my preface to The Tarot of the Bohemians I have mentioned that the first writer who made known the fact of the cards was the archaeologist Court de Gebelin, who, just prior to the French Revolution, occupied several years in the publication of his Monde Primitif, which extended to nine quarto volumes. He was a learned man of his epoch, a high-grade Mason, a member of the historical Lodge of the Philalethes, and a virtuoso with a profound and lifelong interest in the debate on universal antiquities before a science of the subject existed. Even at this day, his memorials and dissertations, collected under the title which I have quoted, are worth possessing. By an accident of things, he became acquainted with the Tarot when it was quite unknown in

Paris, and at once conceived that it was the remnants of an Egyptian book. He made inquiries concerning it and ascertained that it was in circulation over a considerable part of Europe—Spain, Italy, Germany and the South of France. It was in use as a game of chance or skill, after the ordinary manner of playing-cards; and he ascertained further how the game was played. But it was in use also for the higher purpose of divination or fortune-telling, and with the help of a learned friend he discovered the significance attributed to the cards, together with the method of arrangement adopted for this purpose. In a word, he made a distinct contribution to our knowledge, and he is still a source of reference—but it is on the question of fact only, and not on the beloved hypothesis that the Tarot contains pure Egyptian doctrine. However, he set the opinion which is prevalent to this day throughout the occult schools, that in the mystery and wonder, the strange night of the gods, the unknown tongue and the undeciphered hieroglyphics which symbolized Egypt at the end of the eighteenth century, the origin of the cards was lost. So dreamed one of the characteristic literati of France, and one can almost understand and sympathize, for the country about the Delta and the Nile was beginning to loom largely in the preoccupation of learned thought, and omne ignolum pro Aegyptiaco was the way of delusion to which many minds tended. It was excusable enough then, but that the madness has continued and, within the charmed circle of the occult sciences, still passes from mouth to mouth—there is no excuse for this. Let us see, therefore, the evidence produced by M. Court de Gebelin in support of his thesis, and, that I may deal justly, it shall be summarized as far as possible in his own words.

(1) The figures and arrangement of the game are manifestly allegorical; (2) the allegories are in

conformity with the civil, philosophical and religious doctrine of ancient Egypt; (3) if the cards were modern, no High Priestess would be included among the Greater Arcana; (4) the figure in question bears the horns of Isis; (5) the card which is called the Emperor has a sceptre terminating in a triple cross; (6) the card entitled the Moon, who is Isis, shews drops of rain or dew in the act of being shed by the luminary and these-as we have seen-are the tears of Isis, which swelled the waters of the Nile and fertilized the fields of Egypt; (7) the seventeenth card, or Star, is the dog-star, Sirius, which was consecrated to Isis and symbolized the opening of the year; (8) the game played with the Tarot is founded on the sacred number seven, which was of great importance in Egypt; (9) the word Tarot is pure Egyptian, in which language Tar=way or road, and Ro=king or royal—it signifies therefore the Royal Road of Life; (10) alternatively, it is derived from A=doctrine Rosh= Mercury =Thoth, and the article T; in sum, Tarosh; and therefore the Tarot is the Book of Thoth, or the Table of the Doctrine of Mercury.

Such is the testimony, it being understood that I have set aside several casual statements, for which no kind of justification is produced. These, therefore, are ten pillars which support the edifice of the thesis, and the same are pillars of sand. The Tarot is, of course, allegorical—that is to say, it is symbolism—but allegory and symbol are catholic—of all countries, nations and times they are not more Egyptian than Mexican they are of Europe and Cathay, of Tibet beyond the Himalayas and of the London gutters. As allegory and symbol, the cards correspond to many types of ideas and things; they are universal and not particular; and the fact that they do not especially and peculiarly respond to Egyptian doctrine—religious, philosophical or civil—is clear from the failure of Court de Gebelin to go further than the affirmation. The presence of a High Priestess among the Trumps Major is more easily explained as the memorial of some popular superstition—that worship of Diana, for example, the persistence of which in modern Italy has been traced with such striking results by Leland. We have also to remember the universality of horns in every cultus, not excepting that of Tibet. The triple cross is preposterous as an instance of Egyptian symbolism; it is the cross of the patriarchal see, both Greek and Latin—of Venice, of Jerusalem, for example—and it is the form of signing used to this day by the priests and laity of the Orthodox Rite. I pass over the idle allusion to the tears of Isis, because other occult writers have told us that they are Hebrew Jods; as regards the seventeenth card, it is the star Sirius or another, as predisposition pleases; the number seven was certainly important in Egypt and any treatise on numerical mysticism will shew that the same statement applies everywhere, even if we elect to ignore the seven Christian Sacraments and the Gifts of the Divine Spirit. Finally, as regards the etymology of the word Tarot, it is sufficient to observe that it was offered before the discovery of the Rosetta Stone and when there was no knowledge of the Egyptian language.

    The thesis of Court de Gebelin was not suffered to repose undisturbed in the mind of the age, appealing to the learned exclusively by means of a quarto volume. It created the opportunity of Tarot cards in Paris, as the centre of France and all things French in the universe. The suggestion that divination by cards had behind it the unexpected warrants of ancient hidden science, and that the root of the whole subject was in the wonder and mystery of Egypt, reflected thereon almost a divine dignity; out of the purlieus of occult practices cartomancy emerged into fashion and assumed for the moment almost pontifical vestures. The first to undertake the role of bateleur, magician and juggler, was the illiterate but zealous adventurer, Alliette; the second, as a kind of High Priestess, full of intuitions and revelations, was Mlle. Lenormand—but she belongs to a later period; while lastly came Julia Orsini, who is referable to a Queen of Cups rather in the tatters of clairvoyance. I am not concerned with these people as tellers of fortune, when destiny itself was shuffling and cutting cards for the game of universal revolution, or for such courts and courtiers as were those of Louis XVIII, Charles IX and Louis Philippe. But under the occult designation of Etteilla, the transliteration of name, Alliette, that perruquier took himself with high seriousness and posed rather as a priest of the occult sciences than as an ordinary adept in l'art de tirer les cartes. Even at this day there are people, like Dr. Papus, who have sought to save some part of his bizarre system from oblivion.

The long and heterogeneous story of Le Monde Primitif had come to the end of its telling in 1782, and in 1783 the tracts of Etteilla had begun pouring from the press, testifying that already he had spent thirty, nay, almost forty years in the study of Egyptian magic, and that he had found the final keys. They were, in fact, the Keys of the Tarot, which was a book of philosophy and the Book of Thoth, but at the same time it was actually written by seventeen Magi in a Temple of Fire, on the borders of the Levant, some three leagues from Memphis. It contained the science of the universe, and the cartomancist proceeded to apply it to Astrology, Alchemy, and fortune-telling, without the slightest diffidence or reserve as to the fact that he was driving a trade. I have really little doubt that he considered it genuine as a metier, and that he himself was the first person whom he convinced concerning his system. But the point which we have to notice is that in this manner was the antiquity of the Tarot generally trumpeted forth. The little books of Etteilla are proof positive that he did not know even his own language; when in the course of time he produced a reformed Tarot, even those who think of him tenderly admit that he spoiled its symbolism; and in respect of antiquities he had only Court de Gebelin as his universal authority.

The cartomancists succeeded one another in the manner which I have mentioned, and of course there were rival adepts of these less than least mysteries; but the scholarship of the subject, if it can be said to have come into existence, reposed after all in the quarto of Court de Gebelin for something more than sixty years. On his authority, there is very little doubt that everyone who became acquainted, by theory or practice, by casual or special concern, with the question of Tarot cards, accepted their Egyptian character. It is said that people are taken commonly at their own valuation, and—following as it does the line of least resistance—the unsolicitous general mind assuredly accepts archaeological pretensions in the sense of their own daring and of those who put them forward. The first who appeared to reconsider the subject with some presumptive titles to a hearing was the French writer Duchesne, but I am compelled to pass him over with a mere reference, and so also some interesting researches on the general subject of playing-cards by Singer in England. The latter believed that the old Venetian game called Trappola was the earliest European form of card-playing, that it was of Arabian origin, and that the fifty-two cards used for the purpose derived from that region. I do not gather that any importance was ever attached to this view.

Duchesne and Singer were followed by another English writer, W. A. Chatto, who reviewed the available facts and the cloud of speculations which had already arisen on the subject. This was in 1848, and his work has still a kind of standard authority, but—after every allowance for a certain righteousness attributable to the independent mind—it remains an indifferent and even a poor performance. It was, however, characteristic in its way of the approaching middle night of the nineteenth century. Chatto rejected the Egyptian hypothesis, but as he was at very little pains concerning it, he would scarcely be held to displace Court de Gebelin if the latter had any firm ground beneath his hypothesis. In 1854 another French writer, Boiteau, took up the general question, maintaining the oriental origin of Tarot cards, though without attempting to prove it. I am not certain, but I think that he is the first writer who definitely identified them with the Gipsies; for him, however, the original Gipsy home was in India, and Egypt did not therefore enter into his calculation.

In 1860 there arose Eliphas Levi, a brilliant and profound illumine whom it is impossible to accept, and with whom it is even more impossible to dispense. There was never a mouth declaring such great things, of all the western voices which have proclaimed or interpreted the science called occult and the doctrine called magical. I suppose that, fundamentally speaking, he cared as much and as little as I do for the phenomenal part, but he explained the phenomena with the assurance of one who openly regarded charlatanry as a great means to an end, if used in a right cause. He came unto his own and his own received him, also at his proper valuation, as a man of great learning—which he never was—and as a revealer of all mysteries without having been received into any. I do not think that there was ever an instance of a writer with greater gifts, after their particular kind, who put them to such indifferent uses. After all, he was only Etteilla a second time in the flesh, endowed in his transmutation with a mouth of gold and a wider casual knowledge. This notwithstanding, he has written the most comprehensive, brilliant, enchanting History of Magic which has ever been drawn into writing in any language. The Tarot and the de Gebelin hypothesis he took into his heart of hearts, and all occult France and all esoteric Britain, Martinists, half-instructed Kabalists, schools of soi disant theosophy—there, here and everywhere—have accepted his judgment about it with the same confidence as his interpretations of those great classics of Kabalism which he had skimmed rather than read. The Tarot for him was not only the most perfect instrument of divination and the keystone of occult science, but it was the primitive book, the sole book of the ancient Magi, the miraculous volume which inspired all the sacred writings of antiquity. In his first work Levi was content, however, with accepting the construction of Court de Gebelin and reproducing the seventh Trump Major with a few Egyptian characteristics. The question of Tarot transmission through the Gipsies did not occupy him, till J. A. Vaillant, a bizarre writer with great knowledge of the Romany people, suggested it in his work on those wandering tribes. The two authors were almost coincident and reflected one another thereafter. It remained for Romain Merlin, in 1869, to point out what should have been obvious, namely, that cards of some kind were known in Europe prior to the arrival of the Gipsies in or about 1417. But as this was their arrival at Luneburg, and as their presence can be traced antecedently, the correction loses a considerable part of its force; it is safer, therefore, to say that the evidence for the use of the Tarot by Romany tribes was not suggested till after the year 1840; the fact that some Gipsies before this period were found using cards is quite explicable on the hypothesis not that they brought them into Europe but found them there already and added them to their stock-in-trade.

We have now seen that there is no particle of evidence for the Egyptian origin of Tarot cards. Looking in other directions, it was once advanced on native authority that cards of some kind were invented in China about the year A.D. 1120. Court de Gebelin believed in his zeal that he had traced them to a Chinese inscription of great imputed antiquity which was said to refer to the subsidence of the waters of the Deluge. The characters of this inscription were contained in seventy-seven compartments, and this constitutes the analogy. India had also its tablets, whether cards or otherwise, and these have suggested similar slender similitudes. But the existence, for example, of ten suits or styles, of twelve numbers each, and representing the avatars of Vishnu as a fish, tortoise, boar, lion, monkey, hatchet, umbrella or bow, as a goat, a boodh and as a horse, in fine, are not going to help us towards the origin of our own Trumps Major, nor do crowns and harps—nor even the presence of possible coins as a synonym of deniers and perhaps as an equivalent of pentacles—do much to elucidate the Lesser Arcana. If every tongue and people and clime and period possessed their cards—if with these also they philosophized, divined and gambled—the fact would be interesting enough, but unless they were Tarot cards, they would illustrate only the universal tendency of man to be pursuing the same things in more or less the same way.

I end, therefore, the history of this subject by repeating that it has no history prior to the fourteenth century, when the first rumours, were heard concerning cards. They may have existed for centuries, but this period would be early enough, if they were only intended for people to try their luck at gambling or their luck at seeing the future; on the other hand, if they contain the deep intimations of Secret Doctrine, then the fourteenth century is again early enough, or at least in this respect we are getting as much as we can.

Part 2
The Doctrine Behind The Veil

The Tarot and Secret Tradition

THE Tarot embodies symbolical presentations of universal ideas, behind which lie all the implicits of the human mind, and it is in this sense that they contain secret doctrine, which is the realization by the few of truths imbedded in the consciousness of all, though they have not passed into express recognition by ordinary men. The theory is that this doctrine has always existed—that is to say, has been excogitated in the consciousness of an elect minority; that it has been perpetuated in secrecy from one to another and has been recorded in secret literatures, like those of Alchemy and Kabalism; that it is contained also in those Instituted Mysteries of which Rosicrucianism offers an example near to our hand in the past, and Craft Masonry a living summary, or general memorial, for those who can interpret its real meaning. Behind the Secret Doctrine it is held that there is an experience or practice by which the Doctrine is justified. It is obvious that in a handbook like the present I can do little more than state the claims, which, however, have been discussed at length in several of my other writings, while it is designed to treat two of its more important phases in books devoted to the Secret Tradition in Freemasonry and in Hermetic literature. As regards Tarot claims, it should be remembered that some considerable part of the imputed Secret Doctrine has been presented in the pictorial emblems of Alchemy, so that the imputed Book of Thoth is in no sense a solitary device of this emblematic kind. Now, Alchemy had two branches, as I have explained fully elsewhere, and the pictorial emblems which I have mentioned are common to both divisions. Its material side is represented in the strange symbolism of the Mutus Liber, printed in the great folios of Mangetus. There the process for the performance of the great work of transmutation is depicted in fourteen copper-plate engravings, which exhibit the different stages of the matter in the various chemical vessels. Above these vessels there are mythological, planetary, solar and lunar symbols, as if the powers and virtues which -according to Hermetic teaching—preside over the development and perfection of the metallic kingdom were intervening actively to assist the two operators who are toiling below. The operators—curiously enough—are male and female. The spiritual side of Alchemy is set forth in the much stranger emblems of the Book of Lambspring, and of this I have already given a preliminary interpretation, to which the reader may be referred.[1] The tract contains the mystery of what is called the mystical or arch-natural elixir, being the marriage of the soul and the spirit in the body of the adept philosopher and the transmutation of the body as the physical result of this marriage. I have never met with more curious intimations than in this one little work. It may be mentioned as a point of fact that both tracts are very much later in time than the latest date that could be assigned to the general distribution of Tarot cards in Europe by the most drastic form of criticism.

[1. See the Occult Review, vol. viii, 1908].

They belong respectively to the end of the seventeenth and sixteenth centuries. As I am not drawing here on the font of imagination to refresh that of fact and experience, I do not suggest that the Tarot set the example of expressing Secret Doctrine in pictures and that it was followed by Hermetic writers; but it is noticeable that it is perhaps the earliest example of this art. It is also the most catholic, because it is not, by attribution or otherwise, a derivative of any one school or literature of occultism; it is not of Alchemy or Kabalism or Astrology or Ceremonial Magic; but, as I have said, it is the presentation of universal ideas by means of universal types, and it is in the combination of these types—if anywhere—that it presents Secret Doctrine.

That combination may, ex hypothesi, reside in the numbered sequence of its series or in their fortuitous assemblage by shuffling, cutting and dealing, as in ordinary games of chance played with cards. Two writers have adopted the first view without prejudice to the second, and I shall do well, perhaps, to dispose at once of what they have said. Mr. MacGregor Mathers, who once published a pamphlet on the Tarot, which was in the main devoted to fortune-telling, suggested that the twenty-two Trumps Major could be constructed, following their numerical order, into what he called a "connected sentence." It was, in fact, the heads of a moral thesis on the human will, its enlightenment by science, represented by the Magician, its manifestation by action—a significance attributed to the High Priestess-its realization (the Empress) in deeds of mercy and beneficence, which qualities were allocated to the Emperor. He spoke also in the familiar conventional manner of prudence, fortitude, sacrifice, hope and ultimate happiness. But if this were the message of the cards, it is certain that there would be no excuse for publishing them at this day or taking the pains to elucidate them at some length. In his Tarot of the Bohemians, a work written with zeal and enthusiasm, sparing no pains of thought or research within its particular lines-but unfortunately without real insight—Dr. Papus has given a singularly elaborate scheme of the Trumps Major. It depends, like that of Mr. Mathers, from their numerical sequence, but exhibits their interrelation in the Divine World, the Macrocosm and Microcosm. In this manner we get, as it were, a spiritual history of man, or of the soul coming out from the Eternal, passing into the darkness of the material body, and returning to the height. I think that the author is here within a measurable distance of the right track, and his views are to this extent informing, but his method—in some respects-confuses the issues and the modes and planes of being.

The Trumps Major have also been treated in the alternative method which I have mentioned, and Grand Orient, in his Manual of Cartomancy, under the guise of a mode of transcendental divination, has really offered the result of certain illustrative readings of the cards when arranged as the result of a fortuitous combination by means of shuffling and dealing. The use of divinatory methods, with whatsoever intention and for whatever purpose, carries with it two suggestions. It may be thought that the deeper meanings are imputed rather than real, but this is disposed of by the fact of certain cards, like the Magician, the High Priestess, the Wheel of Fortune, the Hanged Man, the Tower or Maison Dieu, and several others, which do not correspond to Conditions of Life, Arts, Sciences, Virtues, or the other subjects contained in the denaries of the Baldini emblematic figures. They are also proof positive that obvious and natural moralities cannot explain the sequence. Such cards testify concerning themselves after another manner; and although the state in which I have left the Tarot in respect of its historical side is so much the more difficult as it is so much the more open, they indicate the real subject matter with which we are concerned. The methods shew also that the Trumps Major at least have been adapted to fortune-telling rather than belong thereto. The common divinatory meanings which will be given in the third part are largely arbitrary attributions, or the product of secondary and uninstructed intuition; or, at the very most, they belong to the subject on a lower plane, apart from the original intention. If the Tarot were of fortune-telling in the root-matter thereof, we should have to look in very strange places for the motive which devised it—to Witchcraft and the Black Sabbath, rather than any Secret Doctrine.

The two classes of significance which are attached to the Tarot in the superior and inferior worlds, and the fact that no occult or other writer has attempted to assign anything but a divinatory meaning to the Minor Arcana, justify in yet another manner the hypothesis that the two series do not belong to one another. It is possible that their marriage was effected first in the Tarot of Bologna by that Prince of Pisa whom I have mentioned in the first part. It is said that his device obtained for him public recognition and reward from the city of his adoption, which would scarcely have been possible, even in those fantastic days, for the production of a Tarot which only omitted a few of the small cards; but as we are dealing with a question of fact which has to be accounted for somehow, it is conceivable that a sensation might have been created by a combination of the minor and gambling cards with the philosophical set, and by the adaptation of both to a game of chance. Afterwards it would have been further adapted to that other game of chance which is called fortune-telling. It should be understood here that I am not denying the possibility of divination, but I take exception as a mystic to the dedications which bring people into these paths, as if they had any relation to the Mystic Quest.

The Tarot cards which are issued with the small edition of the present work, that is to say, with the Key to the Tarot, have been drawn and coloured by Miss Pamela Colman Smith, and will, I think, be regarded as very striking and beautiful, in their design alike and execution. They are reproduced in the present enlarged edition of the Key as a means of reference to the text. They differ in many important respects from the conventional archaisms of the past and from the wretched products of colportage which now reach us from Italy, and it remains for me to justify their variations so far as the symbolism is concerned. That for once in modern times I present a pack which is the work of an artist does not, I presume, call for apology, even to the people—if any remain among us—who used to be described and to call themselves "very occult." If any one will look at the gorgeous Tarot valet or knave who is emblazoned on one of the page plates of Chatto's Facts and Speculations concerning the History of Playing Cards, he will know that Italy in the old days produced some splendid packs. I could only wish that it had been possible to issue the restored and rectified cards in the same style and size; such a course would have done fuller justice to the designs, but the result would have proved unmanageable for those practical purposes which are connected with cards, and for which allowance must be made, whatever my views thereon. For the variations in the symbolism by which the designs have been affected, I alone am responsible. In respect of the Major Arcana, they are sure to occasion criticism among students, actual and imputed. I wish therefore to say, within the reserves of courtesy and la haute convenance belonging to the fellowship of research, that I care nothing utterly for any view that may find expression. There is a Secret Tradition concerning the Tarot, as well as a Secret Doctrine contained therein; I have followed some part of it without exceeding the limits which are drawn about matters of this kind and belong to the laws of honour. This tradition has two parts, and as one of them has passed into writing it seems to follow that it may be betrayed at any moment, which will not signify, because the second, as I have intimated, has not so passed at present and is held by very few indeed. The purveyors of spurious copy and the traffickers in stolen goods may take note of this point, if they please. I ask, moreover, to be distinguished from two or three writers in recent times who have thought fit to hint that they could say a good deal more if they liked, for we do not speak the same language; but also from any one who, now or hereafter, may say that she or he will tell all, because they have only the accidents and not the essentials necessary for such disclosure. If I have followed on my part the counsel of Robert Burns, by keeping something to myself which I "scarcely tell to any," I have still said as much as I can; it is the truth after its own manner, and as much as may be expected or required in those outer circles where the qualifications of special research cannot be expected.

In regard to the Minor Arcana, they are the first in modern but not in all times to be accompanied by pictures, in addition to what is called the "pips"—that is to say, the devices belonging to the numbers of the various suits. These pictures respond to the divinatory meanings, which have been drawn from many sources. To sum up, therefore, the present division of this key is devoted to the Trumps Major; it elucidates their symbols in respect of the higher intention and with reference to the designs in the pack. The third division will give the divinatory significance in respect of the seventy-eight Tarot cards, and with particular reference to the designs of the Minor Arcana. It will give, in fine, some modes of use for those who require them, and in the sense of the reason which I have already explained in the preface. That which hereinafter follows should be taken, for purposes of comparison, in connexion with the general description of the old Tarot Trumps in the first part. There it will be seen that the zero card of the Fool is allocated, as it always is, to the place which makes it equivalent to the number twenty-one. The arrangement is ridiculous on the surface, which does not much signify, but it is also wrong on the symbolism, nor does this fare better when it is made to replace the twenty-second point of the sequence. Etteilla recognized the difficulties of both attributions, but he only made bad worse by allocating the Fool to the place which is usually occupied by the Ace of Pentacles as the last of the whole Tarot series. This rearrangement has been followed by Papus recently in Le Tarot Divinatoire, where the confusion is of no consequence, as the findings of fortune telling depend upon fortuitous positions and not upon essential place in the general sequence of cards. I have seen yet another allocation of the zero symbol, which no doubt obtains in certain cases, but it fails on the highest planes and for our present requirements it would be idle to carry the examination further.

The Trumps Major and their Inner Symbolism

I. The Magician

A youthful figure in the robe of a magician, having the countenance of divine Apollo, with smile of confidence and shining eyes. Above his head is the mysterious sign of the Holy Spirit, the sign of life, like an endless cord, forming the figure 8 in a horizontal position . About his waist is a serpent-cincture, the serpent appearing to devour its own tail. This is familiar to most as a conventional symbol of eternity, but here it indicates more especially the eternity of attainment in the spirit. In the Magician's right hand is a wand raised towards heaven, while the left hand is pointing to the earth. This dual sign is known in very high grades of the Instituted Mysteries; it shews the descent of grace, virtue and light, drawn from things above and derived to things below. The suggestion throughout is therefore the possession and communication of the Powers and Gifts of the Spirit. On the table in front of the Magician are the symbols of the four Tarot suits, signifying the elements of natural life, which lie like counters before the adept, and he adapts them as he wills. Beneath are roses and lilies, the flos campi and lilium convallium, changed into garden flowers, to shew the culture of aspiration. This card signifies the divine motive in man, reflecting God, the will in the liberation of its union with that which is above. It is also the unity of individual being on all planes, and in a very high sense it is thought, in the fixation thereof. With further reference to what I have called the sign of life and its connexion with the number 8, it may be remembered that Christian Gnosticism speaks of rebirth in Christ as a change "unto the Ogdoad." The mystic number is termed Jerusalem above, the Land flowing with Milk and Honey, the Holy Spirit and the Land of the Lord. According to Martinism, 8 is the number of Christ.

II. The High Priestess

She has the lunar crescent at her feet, a horned diadem on her head, with a globe in the middle place, and a large solar cross on her breast. The scroll in her hands is inscribed with the word Tora, signifying the Greater Law, the Secret Law and the second sense of the Word. It is partly covered by her mantle, to shew that some things are implied and some spoken. She is seated between the white and black pillars—J. and B.—of the mystic Temple, and the veil of the Temple is behind her: it is embroidered with palms and pomegranates. The vestments are flowing and gauzy, and the mantle suggests light—a shimmering radiance. She has been called occult Science on the threshold of the Sanctuary of Isis, but she is really the Secret Church, the House which is of God and man. She represents also the Second Marriage of the Prince who is no longer of this world; she is the spiritual Bride and Mother, the daughter of the stars and the Higher Garden of Eden. She is, in fine, the Queen of the borrowed light, but this is the light of all. She is the Moon nourished by the milk of the Supernal Mother.

In a manner, she is also the Supernal Mother herself—that is to say, she is the bright reflection. It is in this sense of reflection that her truest and highest name in bolism is Shekinah—the co-habiting glory. According to Kabalism, there is a Shekinah both above and below. In the superior world it is called Binah, the Supernal Understanding which reflects to the emanations that are beneath. In the lower world it is Malkuth—that world being, for this purpose, understood as a blessed Kingdom that with which it is made blessed being the Indwelling Glory. Mystically speaking, the Shekinah is the Spiritual Bride of the just man, and when he reads the Law she gives the Divine meaning.

There are some respects in which this card is the highest and holiest of the Greater Arcana.

III. The Empress

A stately figure, seated, having rich vestments and royal aspect, as of a daughter of heaven and earth. Her diadem is of twelve stars, gathered in a cluster. The symbol of Venus is on the shield which rests near her. A field of corn is ripening in front of her, and beyond there is a fall of water. The sceptre which she bears is surmounted by the globe of this world. She is the inferior Garden of Eden, the Earthly Paradise, all that is symbolized by the visible house of man. She is not Regina coeli, but she is still refugium peccatorum, the fruitful mother of thousands. There are also certain aspects in which she has been correctly described as desire and the wings thereof, as the woman clothed with the sun, as Gloria Mundi and the veil of the Sanctum Sanctorum; but she is not, I may add, the soul that has attained wings, unless all the symbolism is counted up another and unusual way. She is above all things universal fecundity and the outer sense of the Word. This is obvious, because there is no direct message which has been given to man like that which is borne by woman; but she does not herself carry its interpretation.

In another order of ideas, the card of the Empress signifies the door or gate by which an entrance is obtained into this life, as into the Garden of Venus; and then the way which leads out therefrom, into that which is beyond, is the secret known to the High Priestess: it is communicated by her to the elect. Most old attributions of this card are completely wrong on the symbolism—as, for example, its identification with the Word, Divine Nature, the Triad, and so forth.

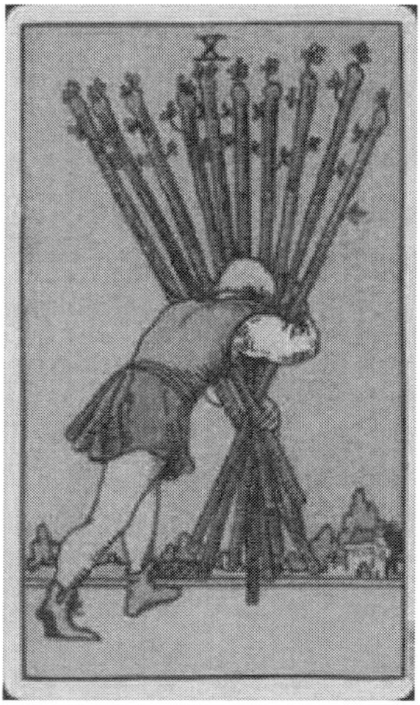
X

IV. The Emperor

He has a form of the Crux ansata for his sceptre and a globe in his left hand. He is a crowned monarch—commanding, stately, seated on a throne, the arms of which axe fronted by rams' heads. He is executive and realization, the power of this world, here clothed with the highest of its natural attributes. He is occasionally represented as seated on a cubic stone, which, however, confuses some of the issues. He is the virile power, to which the Empress responds, and in this sense is he who seeks to remove the Veil of Isis; yet she remains virgo intacta.

It should be understood that this card and that of the Empress do not precisely represent the condition of married life, though this state is implied. On the surface, as I have indicated, they stand for mundane royalty, uplifted on the seats of the mighty; but above this there is the suggestion of another presence. They signify also—and the male figure especially—the higher kingship, occupying the intellectual throne. Hereof is the lordship of thought rather than of the animal world. Both personalities, after their own manner, are "full of strange experience," but theirs is not consciously the wisdom which draws from a higher world. The Emperor has been described as (a) will in its embodied form, but this is only one of its applications, and (b) as an expression of virtualities contained in the Absolute Being—but this is fantasy.

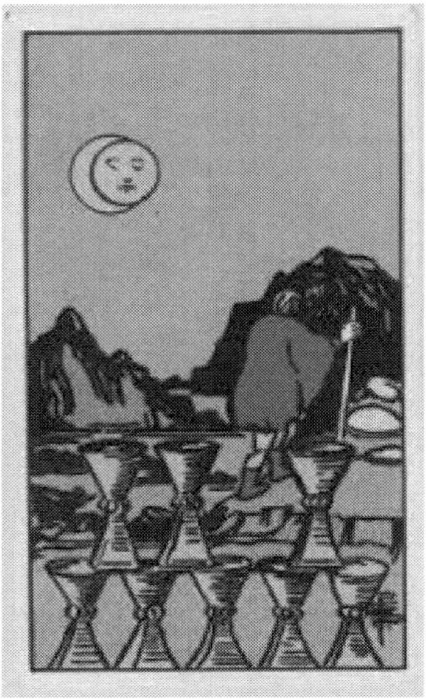

V. The Hierophant

He wears the triple crown and is seated between two pillars, but they are not those of the Temple which is guarded by the High Priestess. In his left hand he holds a sceptre terminating in the triple cross, and with his right hand he gives the well-known ecclesiastical sign which is called that of esotericism, distinguishing between the manifest and concealed part of doctrine. It is noticeable in this connexion that the High Priestess makes no sign. At his feet are the crossed keys, and two priestly ministers in albs kneel before him. He has been usually called the Pope, which is a particular application of the more general office that he symbolizes. He is the ruling power of external religion, as the High Priestess is the prevailing genius of the esoteric, withdrawn power. The proper meanings of this card have suffered woeful admixture from nearly all hands. Grand Orient says truly that the Hierophant is the power of the keys, exoteric orthodox doctrine, and the outer side of the life which leads to the doctrine; but he is certainly not the prince of occult doctrine, as another commentator has suggested.

He is rather the summa totius theologiae, when it has passed into the utmost rigidity of expression; but he symbolizes also all things that are righteous and sacred on the manifest side. As such, he is the channel of grace belonging to the world of institution as distinct from that of Nature, and he is the leader of salvation for the human race at large. He is the order and the head of the recognized hierarchy, which is the reflection of another and greater hierarchic order; but it may so happen that the pontiff forgets the significance of this his symbolic state and acts as if he contained within his proper measures all that his sign signifies or his symbol seeks to shew forth. He is not, as it has been thought, philosophy-except on the theological side; he is not inspiration; and he is not religion, although he is a mode of its expression.

VI. The Lovers

The sun shines in the zenith, and beneath is a great winged figure with arms extended, pouring down influences. In the foreground are two human figures, male and female, unveiled before each other, as if Adam and Eve when they first occupied the paradise of the earthly body. Behind the man is the Tree of Life, bearing twelve fruits, and the Tree of the Knowledge of Good and Evil is behind the woman; the serpent is twining round it. The figures suggest youth, virginity, innocence and love before it is contaminated by gross material desire. This is in all simplicity the card of human love, here exhibited as part of the way, the truth and the life. It replaces, by recourse to first principles, the old card of marriage, which I have described previously, and the later follies which depicted man between vice and virtue. In a very high sense, the card is a mystery of the Covenant and Sabbath.

The suggestion in respect of the woman is that she signifies that attraction towards the sensitive life which carries within it the idea of the Fall of Man, but she is rather the working of a Secret Law of Providence than a willing and conscious temptress. It is through her imputed lapse that man shall arise ultimately, and only by her can he complete himself. The card is therefore in its way another intimation concerning the great mystery of womanhood. The old meanings fall to pieces of necessity with the old pictures, but even as interpretations of the latter, some of them were of the order of commonplace and others were false in symbolism.

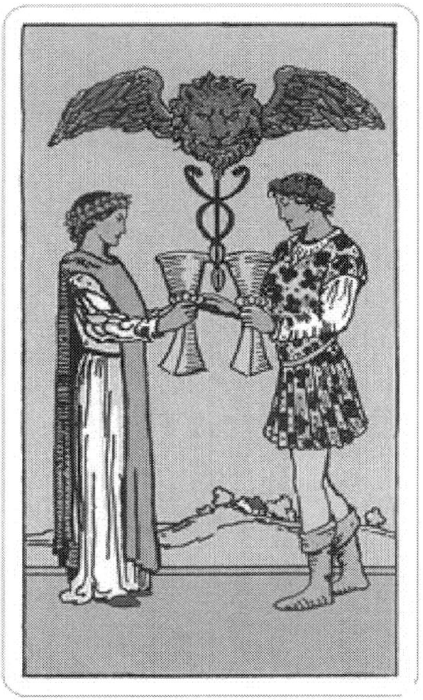

VII. The Chariot

An erect and princely figure carrying a drawn sword and corresponding, broadly speaking, to the traditional description which I have given in the first part. On the shoulders of the victorious hero are supposed to be the Urim and Thummim. He has led captivity captive; he is conquest on all planes—in the mind, in science, in progress, in certain trials of initiation. He has thus replied to the sphinx, and it is on this account that I have accepted the variation of Eliphas Levi; two sphinxes thus draw his chariot. He is above all things triumph in the mind.

It is to be understood for this reason (a) that the question of the sphinx is concerned with a Mystery of Nature and not of the world of Grace, to which the charioteer could offer no answer; (b) that the planes of his conquest are manifest or external and not within himself; (c) that the liberation which he effects may leave himself in the bondage of the logical understanding; (d) that the tests of initiation through which he has passed in triumph are to be understood physically or rationally; and (e) that if he came to the pillars of that Temple between which the High Priestess is seated, he could not open the scroll called Tora, nor if she questioned him could he answer. He is not hereditary royalty and he is not priesthood.

VIII. Strength, or Fortitude

A woman, over whose head there broods the same symbol of life which we have seen in the card of the Magician, is closing the jaws of a lion. The only point in which this design differs from the conventional presentations is that her beneficent fortitude has already subdued the lion, which is being led by a chain of flowers. For reasons which satisfy myself, this card has been interchanged with that of justice, which is usually numbered eight. As the variation carries nothing with it which will signify to the reader, there is no cause for explanation. Fortitude, in one of its most exalted aspects, is connected with the Divine Mystery of Union; the virtue, of course, operates in all planes, and hence draws on all in its symbolism. It connects also with innocentia inviolata, and with the strength which resides in contemplation.

These higher meanings are, however, matters of inference, and I do not suggest that they are transparent on the surface of the card. They are intimated in a concealed manner by the chain of flowers, which signifies, among many other things, the sweet yoke and the light burden of Divine Law, when it has been taken into the heart of hearts. The card has nothing to do with self-confidence in the ordinary sense, though this has been suggested—but it concerns the confidence of those whose strength is God, who have found their refuge in Him. There is one aspect in which the lion signifies the passions, and she who is called Strength is the higher nature in its liberation. It has walked upon the asp and the basilisk and has trodden down the lion and the dragon.

IX. The Hermit

The variation from the conventional models in this card is only that the lamp is not enveloped partially in the mantle of its bearer, who blends the idea of the Ancient of Days with the Light of the World It is a star which shines in the lantern. I have said that this is a card of attainment, and to extend this conception the figure is seen holding up his beacon on an eminence. Therefore the Hermit is not, as Court de Gebelin explained, a wise man in search of truth and justice; nor is he, as a later explanation proposes, an especial example of experience. His beacon intimates that "where I am, you also may be."

It is further a card which is understood quite incorrectly when it is connected with the idea of occult isolation, as the protection of personal magnetism against admixture. This is one of the frivolous renderings which we owe to Eliphas Levi. It has been adopted by the French Order of Martinism and some of us have heard a great deal of the Silent and Unknown Philosophy enveloped by his mantle from the knowledge of the profane. In true Martinism, the significance of the term Philosophe inconnu was of another order. It did not refer to the intended concealment of the Instituted Mysteries, much less of their substitutes, but—like the card itself—to the truth that the Divine Mysteries secure their own protection from those who are unprepared.

X. Wheel of Fortune

In this symbol I have again followed the reconstruction of Eliphas Levi, who has furnished several variants. It is legitimate—as I have intimated—to use Egyptian symbolism when this serves our purpose, provided that no theory of origin is implied therein. I have, however, presented Typhon in his serpent form. The symbolism is, of course, not exclusively Egyptian, as the four Living Creatures of Ezekiel occupy the angles of the card, and the wheel itself follows other indications of Levi in respect of Ezekiel's vision, as illustrative of the particular Tarot Key. With the French occultist, and in the design itself, the symbolic picture stands for the perpetual motion of a fluidic universe and for the flux of human life. The Sphinx is the equilibrium therein. The transliteration of Taro as Rota is inscribed on the wheel, counterchanged with the letters of the Divine Name—to shew that Providence is imphed through all. But this is the Divine intention within, and the similar intention without is exemplified by the four Living Creatures. Sometimes the sphinx is represented couchant on a pedestal above, which defrauds the symbolism by stultifying the essential idea of stability amidst movement.

Behind the general notion expressed in the symbol there lies the denial of chance and the fatality which is implied therein. It may be added that, from the days of Levi onward, the occult explanations of this card are—even for occultism itself—of a singularly fatuous kind. It has been said to mean principle, fecundity, virile honour, ruling authority, etc. The findings of common fortune-telling are better than this on their own plane.

XI. Justice

As this card follows the traditional symbolism and carries above all its obvious meanings, there is little to say regarding it outside the few considerations collected in the first part, to which the reader is referred.

It will be seen, however, that the figure is seated between pillars, like the High Priestess, and on this account it seems desirable to indicate that the moral principle which deals unto every man according to his works—while, of course, it is in strict analogy with higher things;—differs in its essence from the spiritual justice which is involved in the idea of election. The latter belongs to a mysterious order of Providence, in virtue of which it is possible for certain men to conceive the idea of dedication to the highest things. The operation of this is like the breathing of the Spirit where it wills, and we have no canon of criticism or ground of explanation concerning it. It is analogous to the possession of the fairy gifts and the high gifts and the gracious gifts of the poet: we have them or have not, and their presence is as much a mystery as their absence. The law of Justice is not however involved by either alternative. In conclusion, the pillars of Justice open into one world and the pillars of the High Priestess into another.

XII. The Hanged Man

The gallows from which he is suspended forms a Tau cross, while the figure—from the position of the legs—forms a fylfot cross. There is a nimbus about the head of the seeming martyr. It should be noted (1) that the tree of sacrifice is living wood, with leaves thereon; (2) that the face expresses deep entrancement, not suffering; (3) that the figure, as a whole, suggests life in suspension, but life and not death. It is a card of profound significance, but all the significance is veiled. One of his editors suggests that Eliphas Levi did not know the meaning, which is unquestionable nor did the editor himself. It has been called falsely a card of martyrdom, a card a of prudence, a card of the Great Work, a card of duty; but we may exhaust all published interpretations and find only vanity. I will say very simply on my own part that it expresses the relation, in one of its aspects, between the Divine and the Universe.

He who can understand that the story of his higher nature is imbedded in this symbolism will receive intimations concerning a great awakening that is possible, and will know that after the sacred Mystery of Death there is a glorious Mystery of Resurrection.

XIII. Death

The veil or mask of life is perpetuated in change, transformation and passage from lower to higher, and this is more fitly represented in the rectified Tarot by one of the apocalyptic visions than by the crude notion of the reaping skeleton. Behind it lies the whole world of ascent in the spirit. The mysterious horseman moves slowly, bearing a black banner emblazoned with the Mystic Rose, which signifies life. Between two pillars on the verge of the horizon there shines the sun of immortality. The horseman carries no visible weapon, but king and child and maiden fall before him, while a prelate with clasped hands awaits his end.

There should be no need to point out that the suggestion of death which I have made in connection with the previous card is, of course, to be understood mystically, but this is not the case in the present instance. The natural transit of man to the next stage of his being either is or may be one form of his progress, but the exotic and almost unknown entrance, while still in this life, into the state of mystical death is a change in the form of consciousness and the passage into a state to which ordinary death is neither the path nor gate. The existing occult explanations of the 13th card are, on the whole, better than usual, rebirth, creation, destination, renewal, and the rest.

XIV. Temperance

A winged angel, with the sign of the sun upon his forehead and on his breast the square and triangle of the septenary. I speak of him in the masculine sense, but the figure is neither male nor female. It is held to be pouring the essences of life from chalice to chalice. It has one foot upon the earth and one upon waters, thus illustrating the nature of the essences. A direct path goes up to certain heights on the verge of the horizon, and above there is a great light, through which a crown is seen vaguely. Hereof is some part of the Secret of Eternal Life, as it is possible to man in his incarnation. All the conventional emblems are renounced herein.

So also are the conventional meanings, which refer to changes in the seasons, perpetual movement of life and even the combination of ideas. It is, moreover, untrue to say that the figure symbolizes the genius of the sun, though it is the analogy of solar light, realized in the third part of our human triplicity. It is called Temperance fantastically, because, when the rule of it obtains in our consciousness, it tempers, combines and harmonises the psychic and material natures. Under that rule we know in our rational part something of whence we came and whither we are going.

XV. The Devil

The design is an accommodation, mean or harmony, between several motives mentioned in the first part. The Horned Goat of Mendes, with wings like those of a bat, is standing on an altar. At the pit of the stomach there is the sign of Mercury. The right hand is upraised and extended, being the reverse of that benediction which is given by the Hierophant in the fifth card. In the left hand there is a great flaming torch, inverted towards the earth. A reversed pentagram is on the forehead. There is a ring in front of the altar, from which two chains are carried to the necks of two figures, male and female. These are analogous with those of the fifth card, as if Adam and Eve after the Fall. Hereof is the chain and fatality of the material life.

The figures are tailed, to signify the animal nature, but there is human intelligence in the faces, and he who is exalted above them is not to be their master for ever. Even now, he is also a bondsman, sustained by the evil that is in him and blind to the liberty of service. With more than his usual derision for the arts which he pretended to respect and interpret as a master therein, Eliphas Levi affirms that the Baphometic figure is occult science and magic. Another commentator says that in the Divine world it signifies predestination, but there is no correspondence in that world with the things which below are of the brute. What it does signify is the Dweller on the Threshold without the Mystical Garden when those are driven forth therefrom who have eaten the forbidden fruit.

XVI. The Tower

Occult explanations attached to this card are meagre and mostly disconcerting. It is idle to indicate that it depicts min in all its aspects, because it bears this evidence on the surface. It is said further that it contains the first allusion to a material building, but I do not conceive that the Tower is more or less material than the pillars which we have met with in three previous cases. I see nothing to warrant Papus in supposing that it is literally the fall of Adam, but there is more in favour of his alternative—that it signifies the materialization of the spiritual word. The bibliographer Christian imagines that it is the downfall of the mind, seeking to penetrate the mystery of God. I agree rather with Grand Orient that it is the ruin of the House of We, when evil has prevailed therein, and above all that it is the rending of a House of Doctrine. I understand that the reference is, however, to a House of Falsehood. It illustrates also in the most comprehensive way the old truth that "except the Lord build the house, they labour in vain that build it."

There is a sense in which the catastrophe is a reflection from the previous card, but not on the side of the symbolism which I have tried to indicate therein. It is more correctly a question of analogy; one is concerned with the fall into the material and animal state, while the other signifies destruction on the intellectual side. The Tower has been spoken of as the chastisement of pride and the intellect overwhelmed in the attempt to penetrate the Mystery of God; but in neither case do these explanations account for the two persons who are the living sufferers. The one is the literal word made void and the other its false interpretation. In yet a deeper sense, it may signify also the end of a dispensation, but there is no possibility here for the consideration of this involved question.

XVII. The Star

A great, radiant star of eight rays, surrounded by seven lesser stars—also of eight rays. The female figure in the foreground is entirely naked. Her left knee is on the land and her right foot upon the water. She pours Water of Life from two great ewers, irrigating sea and land. Behind her is rising ground and on the right a shrub or tree, whereon a bird alights. The figure expresses eternal youth and beauty. The star is l'etoile flamboyante, which appears in Masonic symbolism, but has been confused therein. That which the figure communicates to the living scene is the substance of the heavens and the elements. It has been said truly that the mottoes of this card are "Waters of Life freely" and "Gifts of the Spirit."

The summary of several tawdry explanations says that it is a card of hope. On other planes it has been certified as immortality and interior light. For the majority of prepared minds, the figure will appear as the type of Truth unveiled, glorious in undying beauty, pouring on the waters of the soul some part and measure of her priceless possession. But she is in reality the Great Mother in the Kabalistic Sephira Binah, which is supernal Understanding, who communicates to the Sephiroth that are below in the measure that they can receive her influx.

XVIII. The Moon

The distinction between this card and some of the conventional types is that the moon is increasing on what is called the side of mercy, to the right of the observer. It has sixteen chief and sixteen secondary rays. The card represents life of the imagination apart from life of the spirit. The path between the towers is the issue into the unknown. The dog and wolf are the fears of the natural mind in the presence of that place of exit, when there is only reflected light to guide it.

The last reference is a key to another form of symbolism. The intellectual light is a reflection and beyond it is the unknown mystery which it cannot shew forth. It illuminates our animal nature, types of which are represented below—the dog, the wolf and that which comes up out of the deeps, the nameless and hideous tendency which is lower than the savage beast. It strives to attain manifestation, symbolized by crawling from the abyss of water to the land, but as a rule it sinks back whence it came. The face of the mind directs a calm gaze upon the unrest below; the dew of thought falls; the message is: Peace, be still; and it may be that there shall come a calm upon the animal nature, while the abyss beneath shall cease from giving up a form.

XIX. The Sun

The naked child mounted on a white horse and displaying a red standard has been mentioned already as the better symbolism connected with this card. It is the destiny of the Supernatural East and the great and holy light which goes before the endless procession of humanity, coming out from the walled garden of the sensitive life and passing on the journey home. The card signifies, therefore, the transit from the manifest light of this world, represented by the glorious sun of earth, to the light of the world to come, which goes before aspiration and is typified by the heart of a child.

But the last allusion is again the key to a different form or aspect of the symbolism. The sun is that of consciousness in the spirit - the direct as the antithesis of the reflected light. The characteristic type of humanity has become a little child therein—a child in the sense of simplicity and innocence in the sense of wisdom. In that simplicity, he bears the seal of Nature and of Art; in that innocence, he signifies the restored world. When the self-knowing spirit has dawned in the consciousness above the natural mind, that mind in its renewal leads forth the animal nature in a state of perfect conformity.

XX. The Last Judgment

I have said that this symbol is essentially invariable in all Tarot sets, or at least the variations do not alter its character. The great angel is here encompassed by clouds, but he blows his bannered trumpet, and the cross as usual is displayed on the banner. The dead are rising from their tombs—a woman on the right, a man on the left hand, and between them their child, whose back is turned. But in this card there are more than three who are restored, and it has been thought worth while to make this variation as illustrating the insufficiency of current explanations. It should be noted that all the figures are as one in the wonder, adoration and ecstacy expressed by their attitudes. It is the card which registers the accomplishment of the great work of transformation in answer to the summons of the Supernal—which summons is heard and answered from within.

Herein is the intimation of a significance which cannot well be carried further in the present place. What is that within us which does sound a trumpet and all that is lower in our nature rises in response—almost in a moment, almost in the twinkling of an eye? Let the card continue to depict, for those who can see no further, the Last judgment and the resurrection in the natural body; but let those who have inward eyes look and discover therewith. They will understand that it has been called truly in the past a card of eternal life, and for this reason it may be compared with that which passes under the name of Temperance.

Zero: The Fool

With light step, as if earth and its trammels had little power to restrain him, a young man in gorgeous vestments pauses at the brink of a precipice among the great heights of the world; he surveys the blue distance before him-its expanse of sky rather than the prospect below. His act of eager walking is still indicated, though he is stationary at the given moment; his dog is still bounding. The edge which opens on the depth has no terror; it is as if angels were waiting to uphold him, if it came about that he leaped from the height. His countenance is full of intelligence and expectant dream. He has a rose in one hand and in the other a costly wand, from which depends over his right shoulder a wallet curiously embroidered. He is a prince of the other world on his travels through this one-all amidst the morning glory, in the keen air. The sun, which shines behind him, knows whence he came, whither he is going, and how he will return by another path after many days. He is the spirit in search of experience. Many symbols of the Instituted Mysteries are summarized in this card, which reverses, under high warrants, all the confusions that have preceded it.

In his Manual of Cartomancy, Grand Orient has a curious suggestion of the office of Mystic Fool, as apart of his process in higher divination; but it might call for more than ordinary gifts to put it into operation. We shall see how the card fares according to the common arts of fortune-telling, and it will be an example, to those who can discern, of the fact, otherwise so evident, that the Trumps Major had no place originally in the arts of psychic gambling, when cards are used as the counters and pretexts. Of the circumstances under which this art arose we know, however, very little. The conventional explanations say that the Fool signifies the flesh, the sensitive life, and by a peculiar satire its subsidiary name was at one time the alchemist, as depicting folly at the most insensate stage.

XXI. The World

As this final message of the Major Trumps is unchanged—and indeed unchangeable—in respect of its design, it has been partly described already regarding its deeper sense. It represents also the perfection and end of the Cosmos, the secret which is within it, the rapture of the universe when it understands itself in God. It is further the state of the soul in the consciousness of Divine Vision, reflected from the self-knowing spirit. But these meanings are without prejudice to that which I have said concerning it on the material side.

It has more than one message on the macrocosmic side and is, for example, the state of the restored world when the law of manifestation shall have been carried to the highest degree of natural perfection. But it is perhaps more especially a story of the past, referring to that day when all was declared to be good, when the morning stars sang together and all the Sons of God shouted for joy. One of the worst explanations concerning it is that the figure symbolizes the Magus when he has reached the highest degree of initiation; another account says that it represents the absolute, which is ridiculous. The figure has been said to stand for Truth, which is, however, more properly allocated to the seventeenth card. Lastly, it has been called the Crown of the Magi.

Conclusion as to the Greater Keys

There has been no attempt in the previous tabulation to present the symbolism in what is called the three worlds—that of Divinity, of the Macrocosm and the Microcosm. A large volume would be required for developments of this kind. I have taken the cards on the high plane of their more direct significance to man, who—in material life—is on the quest of eternal things. The compiler of the Manual of Cartomancy has treated them under three headings: the World of Human Prudence, which does not differ from divination on its more serious side; the World of Conformity, being the life of religious devotion; and the World of Attainment, which is that of "the soul's progress towards the term of its research." He gives also a triple process of consultation, according to these divisions, to which the reader is referred. I have no such process to offer, as I think that more may be gained by individual reflection on each of the Trumps Major. I have also not adopted the prevailing attribution of the cards to the Hebrew alphabet—firstly, because it would serve no purpose in an elementary handbook; secondly, because nearly every attribution is wrong. Finally, I have not attempted to rectify the position of the cards in their relation to one another; the Zero therefore appears after No. 20, but I have taken care not to number the World or Universe otherwise than as 21. Wherever it ought to be put, the Zero is an unnumbered card.

In conclusion as to this part, I will give these further indications regarding the Fool, which is the most speaking of all the symbols. He signifies the journey outward, the state of the first emanation, the graces and passivity of the spirit. His wallet is inscribed with dim signs, to shew that many sub-conscious memories are stored up in the soul.

Part 3
The Outer Method Of The Oracles

Distinction between the Greater and Lesser Arcana

IN respect of their usual presentation, the bridge between the Greater and Lesser Arcana is supplied by the court cards—King, Queen, Knight and Squire or Page; but their utter distinction from the Trumps Major is shewn by their conventional character. Let the reader compare them with symbols like the Fool, the High Priestess, the Hierophant, or—almost without exception—with any in the previous sequence, and he will discern my meaning. There is no especial idea connected on the surface with the ordinary court cards; they are a bridge of conventions, which form a transition to the simple pretexts of the counters and denaries of the numbers following. We seem to have passed away utterly from the region of higher meanings illustrated by living pictures. There in was a period, however, when the numbered cards were also pictures, but such devices were sporadic inventions of particular artists and were either conventional designs of the typical or allegorical kind, distinct from what is understood by symbolism, or they were illustrations—shall we say?—of manners, customs and periods. They were, in a word, adornments, and as such they did nothing to raise the significance of the Lesser Arcana to the plane of the Trumps Major; moreover, such variations are exceedingly few. This notwithstanding, there are vague rumours concerning a higher meaning in the minor cards, but nothing has so far transpired, even within the sphere of prudence which belongs to the most occult circles; these, it is true, have certain variants in respect of divinatory values, but I have not heard that in practice they offer better results. Efforts like those of Papus in The Tarot ol the Bohemians are strenuous and deserving after their own kind; be, in particular, recognizes the elements of the

Divine Immanence in the Trumps Major, and he seeks to follow them through the long series of the lesser cards, as if these represented filtrations of the World of Grace through the World of Fortune; but he only produces -an arbitrary scheme of division which he can carry no further, and he has recourse, of necessity, in the end to a common scheme of divination as the substitute for a title to existence on the part of the Lesser Arcana. Now, I am practically in the same position; but I shall make no attempt here to save the situation by drawing on the mystical properties of numbers, as he and others have attempted, I shall recognize at once that the Trumps Major belong to the divine dealings of philosophy, but all that follows to fortune-telling, since it has never yet been translated into another language; the course thus adopted will render to divination, and at need even to gambling, the things that belong to this particular world of skill, and it will set apart for their proper business those matters that are of another order. In this free introduction to the subject in hand, it is only necessary to add that the difference between the fifty-six Lesser Arcana and ordinary playing-cards is not only essentially slight, because the substitution of Cups for Hearts, and so forth, constitutes an accidental variation, but because the presence of a Knight in each of the four suits was characteristic at one time of many ordinary packs, when this personage usually replaced the Queen. In the rectified Tarot which illustrates the present handbook, all numbered cards of the Lesser Arcana—the Aces only excepted—are furnished with figures or pictures to illustrate-but without exhausting—the divinatory meanings attached thereto.

Some who are gifted with reflective and discerning faculties in more than the ordinary sense—I am not speaking of clairvoyance may observe that in many of the Lesser Arcana there are vague intimations conveyed by the designs which seem to exceed the stated divinatory values. It is desirable to avoid misconception by specifying definitely that, except in rare instances—and then only by accident—the variations are not to be regarded as suggestions of higher and extradivinatory symbolism. I have said that these Lesser Arcana have not been translated into a language which transcends that of fortune telling. I should not indeed be disposed to regard them as belonging in their existing forms to another realm than this; but the field of divinatory possibilities is inexhaustible, by the hypothesis of the art, and the combined systems of cartomancy have indicated only the bare heads of significance attaching to the emblems in use. When the pictures in the present case go beyond the conventional meanings they should be taken as hints of possible developments along the same lines; and this is one of the reasons why the pictorial devices here attached to the four denaries will prove a great help to intuition. The mere numerical powers and bare words of the meanings are insufficient by themselves; but the pictures are like doors which open into unexpected chambers, or like a turn in the open road with a wide prospect beyond.

The Lesser Arcana, otherwise, the Four Suits of Tarot Cards

Otherwise, the Four Suits of Tarot Cards, will now be described according to their respective classes by the pictures to each belonging, and a harmony of their meanings will be provided from all sources.

THE SUIT OF WANDS

King of Wands
The physical and emotional nature to which this card is attributed is dark, ardent, lithe, animated, impassioned, noble. The King uplifts a flowering wand, and wears, like his three correspondences in the remaining suits, what is called a cap of maintenance beneath his crown. He connects with the symbol of the lion, which is emblazoned on the back of his throne. Divinatory Meanings: Dark man, friendly, countryman, generally married, honest and conscientious. The card always signifies honesty, and may mean news concerning an unexpected heritage to fall in before very long. Reversed: Good, but severe; austere, yet tolerant.

Queen of Wands
The Wands throughout this suit are always in leaf, as it is a suit of life and animation. Emotionally and otherwise, the Queen's personality corresponds to that of the King, but is more magnetic. Divinatory Meanings: A dark woman, countrywoman, friendly, chaste, loving, honourable. If the card beside her signifies a man, she is well disposed towards him; if a woman, she is interested in the Querent. Also, love of money, or a certain success in business. Reversed: Good, economical, obliging, serviceable. Signifies also—but in certain positions and

in the neighbourhood of other cards tending in such directions—opposition, jealousy, even deceit and infidelity.

Knight of Wands

He is shewn as if upon a journey, armed with a short wand, and although mailed is not on a warlike errand. He is passing mounds or pyramids. The motion of the horse is a key to the character of its rider, and suggests the precipitate mood, or things connected therewith. Divinatory Meanings: Departure, absence, flight, emigration. A dark young man, friendly. Change of residence. Reversed: Rupture, division, interruption, discord.

Page of Wands

In a scene similar to the former, a young man stands in the act of proclamation. He is unknown but faithful, and his tidings are strange. Divinatory Meanings: Dark young man, faithful, a lover, an envoy, a postman. Beside a man, he will bear favourable testimony concerning him. A dangerous rival, if followed by the Page of Cups. Has the chief qualities of his suit. He may signify family intelligence. Reversed: Anecdotes, announcements, evil news. Also indecision and the instability which accompanies it.

Ten of Wands

A man oppressed by the weight of the ten staves which he is carrying. Divinatory Meanings: A card of many significances, and some of the readings cannot be harmonized. I set aside that which connects it with honour and good faith. The chief meaning is oppression simply, but it is also fortune, gain, any kind of success, and then it is the oppression of these things. It is also a card of false-seeming, disguise, perfidy. The place which the figure is approaching may suffer from the rods that he carries. Success is stultified if the Nine of Swords follows, and if it is a question of a lawsuit, there will be certain loss. Reversed: Contrarieties, difficulties, intrigues, and their analogies.

Nine of Wands

The figure leans upon his staff and has an expectant look, as if awaiting an enemy. Behind are eight other staves—erect, in orderly disposition, like a palisade. Divinatory Meanings: The card signifies strength in opposition. If attacked, the person will meet an onslaught boldly; and his build shews, that he may prove a formidable antagonist. With this main significance there are all its possible adjuncts—delay, suspension, adjournment. Reversed: Obstacles, adversity, calamity.

Eight of Wands

The card represents motion through the immovable-a flight of wands through an open country; but they draw to the term of their course. That which they signify is at hand; it may be even on the threshold. Divinatory Meanings: Activity in undertakings, the path of such activity, swiftness, as that of an express messenger; great haste, great hope, speed towards an end which promises assured felicity; generally, that which is on the move; also the arrows of love. Reversed: Arrows of jealousy, internal dispute, stingings of conscience, quarrels; and domestic disputes for persons who are married.

Seven of Wands

A young man on a craggy eminence brandishing a staff; six other staves are raised towards him from below. Divinatory Meanings: It is a card of valour, for, on the surface, six are attacking one, who has, however, the vantage position. On the intellectual plane, it signifies discussion, wordy strife; in business—negotiations, war of trade, barter, competition. It is further a card of success, for the combatant is on the top and his enemies may be unable to reach him. Reversed: Perplexity, embarrassments, anxiety. It is also a caution against indecision.

Six of Wands

A laurelled horseman bears one staff adorned with a laurel crown; footmen with staves are at his side. Divinatory Meanings: The card has been so designed that it can cover several significations; on the surface, it is a victor triumphing, but it is also great news, such as might be carried in state by the King's courier; it is expectation crowned with its own desire, the crown of hope, and so forth. Reversed: Apprehension, fear, as of a victorious enemy at the gate; treachery, disloyalty, as of gates being opened to the enemy; also indefinite delay.

Five of Wands

A posse of youths, who are brandishing staves, as if in sport or strife. It is mimic warfare, and hereto correspond the Divinatory Meanings: Imitation, as, for example, sham fight, but also the strenuous competition and struggle of the search after riches and fortune. In this sense it connects with the battle of life. Hence some attributions say that it is a card of gold, gain, opulence. Reversed: Litigation, disputes, trickery, contradiction.

Four of Wands

From the four great staves planted in the foreground there is a great garland suspended; two female figures uplift nosegays; at their side is a bridge over a moat, leading to an old manorial house. Divinatory Meanings: They are for once almost on the surface—country life, haven of refuge, a species of domestic harvest-home, repose, concord, harmony, prosperity, peace, and the perfected work of these. Reversed: The meaning remains unaltered; it is prosperity, increase, felicity, beauty, embellishment.

Three of Wands

A calm, stately personage, with his back turned, looking from a cliff's edge at ships passing over the sea. Three staves are planted in the ground, and he leans slightly on one of them. Divinatory Meanings: He symbolizes established strength, enterprise, effort, trade, commerce, discovery; those are his ships, bearing his merchandise, which are sailing over the sea. The card also signifies able co-operation in business, as if the successful merchant prince were looking from his side towards yours with a view to help you. Reversed: The end of troubles, suspension or cessation of adversity, toil and disappointment.

Two of Wands

A tall man looks from a battlemented roof over sea and shore; he holds a globe in his right hand, while a staff in his left rests on the battlement; another is fixed in a ring. The Rose and Cross and Lily should be noticed on the left side. Divinatory Meanings: Between the alternative readings there is no marriage possible; on the one hand, riches, fortune, magnificence; on the other, physical suffering, disease, chagrin, sadness, mortification. The design gives one suggestion; here is a lord overlooking his dominion and alternately contemplating a globe; it looks like the malady, the mortification, the sadness of Alexander amidst the grandeur of this world's wealth. Reversed: Surprise, wonder, enchantment, emotion, trouble, fear.

Ace of Wands

A hand issuing from a cloud grasps a stout wand or club. Divinatory Meanings: Creation, invention, enterprise, the powers which result in these; principle, beginning, source; birth, family, origin, and in a sense the virility which is behind them; the starting point of enterprises; according to another account, money, fortune, inheritance. Reversed: Fall, decadence, ruin, perdition, to perish also a certain clouded joy.

THE SUIT OF CUPS

King of Cups

He holds a short sceptre in his left hand and a great cup in his right; his throne is set upon the sea; on one side a ship is riding and on the other a dolphin is leaping. The implicit is that the Sign of the Cup naturally refers to water, which appears in all the court cards. Divinatory Meanings: Fair man, man of business, law, or divinity; responsible, disposed to oblige the Querent; also equity, art and science, including those who profess science, law and art; creative intelligence. Reversed: Dishonest, double-dealing man; roguery, exaction, injustice, vice, scandal, pillage, considerable loss.

Queen of Cups

Beautiful, fair, dreamy—as one who sees visions in a cup. This is, however, only one of her aspects; she sees, but she also acts, and her activity feeds her dream. Divinatory Meanings: Good, fair woman; honest, devoted woman, who will do service to the Querent; loving intelligence, and hence the gift of vision; success, happiness, pleasure; also wisdom, virtue; a perfect spouse and a good mother. Reversed: The accounts vary; good woman; otherwise, distinguished woman but one not to be trusted; perverse woman; vice, dishonour, depravity.

Knight of Cups

Graceful, but not warlike; riding quietly, wearing a winged helmet, referring to those higher graces of the imagination which sometimes characterize this card. He too is a dreamer, but the images of the side of sense haunt him in his vision. Divinatory Meanings: Arrival, approach—sometimes that of a messenger; advances, proposition, demeanour, invitation, incitement. Reversed: Trickery, artifice, subtlety, swindling, duplicity, fraud.

Page of Cups

A fair, pleasing, somewhat effeminate page, of studious and intent aspect, contemplates a fish rising from a cup to look at him. It is the pictures of the mind taking form. Divinatory Meanings: Fair young man, one impelled to render service and with whom the Querent will be connected; a studious youth; news, message; application, reflection, meditation; also these things directed to business. Reversed: Taste, inclination, attachment, seduction, deception, artifice.

Ten of Cups

Appearance of Cups in a rainbow; it is contemplated in wonder and ecstacy by a man and woman below, evidently husband and wife. His right arm is about her; his left is raised upward; she raises her right arm. The two children dancing near them have not observed the prodigy but are happy after their own manner. There is a home-scene beyond. Divinatory Meanings:

Contentment, repose of the entire heart; the perfection of that state; also perfection of human love and friendship; if with several picture-cards, a person who is taking charge of the Querent's interests; also the town, village or country inhabited by the Querent. Reversed: Repose of the false heart, indignation, violence.

Nine of Cups

A goodly personage has feasted to his heart's content, and abundant refreshment of wine is on the arched counter behind him, seeming to indicate that the future is also assured. The picture offers the material side only, but there are other aspects. Divinatory Meanings: Concord, contentment, physical bien-etre; also victory, success, advantage; satisfaction for the Querent or person for whom the consultation is made. Reversed: Truth, loyalty, liberty; but the readings vary and include mistakes, imperfections, etc.

Eight of Cups

A man of dejected aspect is deserting the cups of his felicity, enterprise, undertaking or previous concern. Divinatory Meanings: The card speaks for itself on the surface, but other readings are entirely antithetical—giving joy, mildness, timidity, honour, modesty. In practice, it is usually found that the card shews the decline of a matter, or that a matter which has been thought to be important is really of slight consequence—either for good or evil. *Reversed*: Great joy, happiness, feasting.

Nine of Cups

A goodly personage has feasted to his heart's content, and abundant refreshment of wine is on the arched counter behind him, seeming to indicate that the future is also assured. The picture offers the material side only, but there are other aspects. Divinatory Meanings: Concord, contentment, physical bien-etre; also victory, success, advantage; satisfaction for the Querent or person for whom the consultation is made. Reversed: Truth, loyalty, liberty; but the readings vary and include mistakes, imperfections, etc.

ing joy, mildness, timidity, honour, modesty. In practice, it is usually found that the card shews the decline of a matter, or that a matter which has been thought to be important is really of slight consequence—either for good or evil. Reversed: Great joy, happiness, feasting.

Seven of Cups

Strange chalices of vision, but the images are more especially those of the fantastic spirit. Divinatory Meanings: Fairy favours, images of reflection, sentiment, imagination, things seen in the glass of contemplation; some attainment in these degrees, but nothing permanent or substantial is suggested. Reversed: Desire, will, determination, project.

Six of Cups

Children in an old garden, their cups filled with flowers. Divinatory Meanings: A card of the past and of memories, looking back, as—for example—on childhood; happiness, enjoyment, but coming rather from the past; things that have vanished. Another reading reverses this, giving new relations, new knowledge, new environment, and then the children are disporting in an unfamiliar precinct. Reversed: The future, renewal, that which will come to pass presently.

Five of Cups

A dark, cloaked figure, looking sideways at three prone cups two others stand upright behind him; a bridge is in the background, leading to a small keep or holding. Divanatory Meanings: It is a card of loss, but something remains over; three have been taken, but two are left; it is a card of inheritance, patrimony, transmission, but not corresponding to expectations; with some interpreters it is a card of marriage, but not without bitterness or frustration. Reversed: News, alliances, affinity, consanguinity, ancestry, return, false projects.

Four of Cups

A young man is seated under a tree and contemplates three cups set on the grass before him; an arm issuing from a cloud offers him another cup. His expression notwithstanding is one of discontent with his environment. Divinatory Meanings: Weariness, disgust, aversion, imaginary vexations, as if the wine of this world had caused satiety only; another wine, as if a fairy gift, is now offered the wastrel, but he sees no consolation therein. This is also a card of blended pleasure. Reversed: Novelty, presage, new instruction, new relations.

Three of Cups

Maidens in a garden-ground with cups uplifted, as if pledging one another. Divinatory Meanings: The conclusion of any matter in plenty, perfection and merriment; happy issue, victory, fulfilment, solace, healing, Reversed: Expedition, dispatch, achievement, end. It signifies also the side of excess in physical enjoyment, and the pleasures of the senses.

Two of Cups

A youth and maiden are pledging one another, and above their cups rises the Caduceus of Hermes, between the great wings of which there appears a lion's head. It is a variant of a sign which is found in a few old examples of this card. Some curious emblematical meanings are attached to it, but they do not concern us in this place. Divinatory Meanings: Love, passion, friendship, affinity, union, concord, sympathy, the interrelation of the sexes, and—as a suggestion apart from all offices of divination—that desire which is not in Nature, but by which Nature is sanctified.

Ace of Cups

The waters are beneath, and thereon are water-lilies; the hand issues from the cloud, holding in its palm the cup, from which four streams are pouring; a dove, bearing in its bill a cross-marked Host, descends to place the Wafer in the Cup; the dew of water is falling on all sides. It is an intimation of that which may lie behind the Lesser Arcana. Divinatory Meanings: House of the true heart, joy, content, abode, nourishment, abundance, fertility; Holy Table, felicity hereof. Reversed: House of the false heart, mutation, instability, revolution.

THE SUIT OF SWORDS

King of Swords

He sits in judgment, holding the unsheathed sign of his suit. He recalls, of course, the conventional Symbol of justice in the Trumps Major, and he may represent this virtue, but he is rather the power of life and death, in virtue of his office. Divinatory Meanings: Whatsoever arises out of the idea of judgment and all its connexions-power, command, authority, militant intelligence, law, offices of the crown, and so forth. Reversed: Cruelty, perversity, barbarity, perfidy, evil intention.

Queen of Swords

Her right hand raises the weapon vertically and the hilt rests on an arm of her royal chair the left hand is extended, the arm raised her countenance is severe but chastened; it suggests familiarity with sorrow. It does not represent mercy, and, her sword notwithstanding, she is scarcely a symbol of power. Divinatory Meanings: Widowhood, female sadness and embarrassment, absence, sterility, mourning, privation, separation. Reversed: Malice, bigotry, artifice, prudery, bale, deceit.

Knight of Swords

He is riding in full course, as if scattering his enemies. In the design he is really a prototypical hero of romantic chivalry. He might almost be Galahad, whose sword is swift and sure because he is clean of heart. Divinatory Meanings: Skill, bravery, capacity, defence, address, enmity, wrath, war, destruction, opposition, resistance, ruin. There is therefore a sense in which the card signifies death, but it carries this meaning only in its proximity to other cards of fatality. Reversed: Imprudence, incapacity, extravagance.

Page of Swords

A lithe, active figure holds a sword upright in both hands, while in the act of swift walking. He is passing over rugged land, and about his way the clouds are collocated wildly. He is alert and lithe, looking this way and that, as if an expected enemy might appear at any moment. Divinatory Meanings: Authority, overseeing, secret service, vigilance, spying, examination, and the qualities thereto belonging. Reversed: More evil side of these qualities; what is unforeseen, unprepared state; sickness is also intimated.

Ten of Swords

A prostrate figure, pierced by all the swords belonging to the card. Divinatory Meanings: Whatsoever is intimated by the design; also pain, affliction, tears, sadness, desolation. It is not especially a card of violent death. Reversed: Advantage, profit, success, favour, but none of these are permanent; also power and authority.

Nine of Swords

One seated on her couch in lamentation, with the swords over her. She is as one who knows no sorrow which is like unto hers. It is a card of utter desolation. Divinatory Meanings: Death, failure, miscarriage, delay, deception, disappointment, despair. Reversed: Imprisonment, suspicion, doubt, reasonable fear, shame.

Eight of Swords

A woman, bound and hoodwinked, with the swords of the card about her. Yet it is rather a card of temporary durance than of irretrievable bondage. Divinatory Meanings: Bad news, violent chagrin, crisis, censure, power in trammels, conflict, calumny; also sickness. Reversed: Disquiet, difficulty, opposition, accident, treachery; what is unforeseen; fatality.

Seven of Swords

A man in the act of carrying away five swords rapidly; the two others of the card remain stuck in the ground. A camp is close at hand. Divinatory Meanings: Design, attempt, wish, hope, confidence; also quarrelling, a plan that may fail, annoyance. The design is uncertain in its import, because the significations are widely at variance with each other. Reversed: Good advice, counsel, instruction, slander, babbling.

Six of Swords

A ferryman carrying passengers in his punt to the further shore. The course is smooth, and seeing that the freight is light, it may be noted that the work is not beyond his strength. Divinatory Meanings: journey by water, route, way, envoy, commissionary, expedient. Reversed: Declaration, confession, publicity; one account says that it is a proposal of love.

Five of Swords

A disdainful man looks after two retreating and dejected figures. Their swords lie upon the ground. He carries two others on his left shoulder, and a third sword is in his right hand, point to earth. He is the master in possession of the field. Divinatory Meanings: Degradation, destruction, revocation, infamy, dishonour, loss, with the variants and analogues of these. Reversed: The same; burial and obsequies.

Four of Swords

The effigy of a knight in the attitude of prayer, at full length upon his tomb. Divinatory Meanings: Vigilance, retreat, solitude, hermit's repose, exile, tomb and coffin. It is these last that have suggested the design. Reversed: Wise administration, circumspection, economy, avarice, precaution, testament.

Three of Swords

Three swords piercing a heart; cloud and rain behind. Divinatory Meanings: Removal, absence, delay, division, rupture, dispersion, and all that the design signifies naturally, being too simple and obvious to call for specific enumeration. Reversed: Mental alienation, error, loss, distraction, disorder, confusion.

Two of Swords

A hoodwinked female figure balances two swords upon her shoulders. Divinatory Meanings: Conformity and the equipoise which it suggests, courage, friendship, concord in a state of arms; another reading gives tenderness, affection, intimacy. The suggestion of harmony and other favourable readings must be considered in a qualified manner, as Swords generally are not symbolical of beneficent forces in human affairs. Reversed: Imposture, falsehood, duplicity, disloyalty.

Ace of Swords

A hand issues from a cloud, grasping as word, the point of which is encircled by a crown. Divinatory Meanings: Triumph, the excessive degree in everything, conquest, triumph of force. It is a card of great force, in love as well as in hatred. The crown may carry a much higher significance than comes usually within the sphere of fortune-telling. Reversed: The same, but the results are disastrous; another account says—conception, childbirth, augmentation, multiplicity.

THE SUIT OF PENTACLES

King of Pentacles

The figure calls for no special description the face is rather dark, suggesting also courage, but somewhat lethargic in tendency. The bull's head should be noted as a recurrent symbol on the throne. The sign of this suit is represented throughout as engraved or blazoned with the pentagram, typifying the correspondence of the four elements in human nature and that by which they may be governed. In many old Tarot packs this suit stood for current coin, money, deniers. I have not invented the substitution of pentacles and I have no special cause to sustain in respect of the alternative. But the consensus of divinatory meanings is on the side of some change, because the cards do not happen to deal especially with questions of money. Divinatory Meanings: Valour, realizing intelligence, business and normal intellectual aptitude, sometimes mathematical gifts and attainments of this kind; success in these paths. Reversed: Vice, weakness, ugliness, perversity, corruption, peril.

Queen of Pentacles

The face suggests that of a dark woman, whose qualities might be summed up in the idea of greatness of soul; she has also the serious cast of intelligence; she contemplates her symbol and may see worlds therein. Divinatory Meanings: Opulence, generosity, magnificence, security, liberty. Reversed: Evil, suspicion, suspense, fear, mistrust.

Knight of Pentacles

He rides a slow, enduring, heavy horse, to which his own aspect corresponds. He exhibits his symbol, but does not look therein. Divinatory Meanings: Utility, serviceableness, interest, responsibility, rectitude-all on the normal and external plane. Reversed: inertia, idleness, repose of that kind, stagnation; also placidity, discouragement, carelessness.

Page of Pentacles

A youthful figure, looking intently at the pentacle which hovers over his raised hands. He moves slowly, insensible of that which is about him. Divinatory Meanings: Application, study, scholarship, reflection another reading says news, messages and the bringer thereof; also rule, management. Reversed: Prodigality, dissipation, liberality, luxury; unfavourable news.

Ten of Pentacles

A man and woman beneath an archway which gives entrance to a house and domain. They are accompanied by a child, who looks curiously at two dogs accosting an ancient personage seated in the foreground. The child's hand is on one of them. Divinatory Meanings: Gain, riches; family matters, archives, extraction, the abode of a family. Reversed: Chance, fatality, loss, robbery, games of hazard; sometimes gift, dowry, pension.

Nine of Pentacles

A woman, with a bird upon her wrist, stands amidst a great abundance of grapevines in the garden of a manorial house. It is a wide domain, suggesting plenty in all things. Possibly it is her own possession and testifies to material well-being. Divinatory Meanings: Prudence, safety, success, accomplishment, certitude, discernment. Reversed: Roguery, deception, voided project, bad faith.

Eight of Pentacles

An artist in stone at his work, which he exhibits in the form of trophies. Divinatory Meanings: Work, employment, commission, craftsmanship, skill in craft and business, perhaps in the preparatory stage. Reversed: Voided ambition, vanity, cupidity, exaction, usury. It may also signify the possession of skill, in the sense of the ingenious mind turned to cunning and intrigue.

Seven of Pentacles

A young man, leaning on his staff, looks intently at seven pentacles attached to a clump of greenery on his right; one would say that these were his treasures and that his heart was there. Divinatory Meanings: These are exceedingly contradictory; in the main, it is a card of money, business, barter; but one reading gives altercation, quarrels—and another innocence, ingenuity, purgation. Reversed: Cause for anxiety regarding money which it may be proposed to lend.

Six of Pentacles

A person in the guise of a merchant weighs money in a pair of scales and distributes it to the needy and distressed. It is a testimony to his own success in life, as well as to his goodness of heart. Divinatory Meanings: Presents, gifts, gratification another account says attention, vigilance now is the accepted time, present prosperity, etc. Reversed: Desire, cupidity, envy, jealousy, illusion.

Five of Pentacles

Two mendicants in a snow-storm pass a lighted casement. Divinatory Meanings: The card foretells material trouble above all, whether in the form illustrated—that is, destitution—or otherwise. For some cartomancists, it is a card of love and lovers-wife, husband, friend, mistress; also concordance, affinities. These alternatives cannot be harmonized. Reversed: Disorder, chaos, ruin, discord, profligacy.

Four of Pentacles

A crowned figure, having a pentacle over his crown, clasps another with hands and arms; two pentacles are under his feet. He holds to that which he has. Divinatory Meanings: The surety of possessions, cleaving to that which one has, gift, legacy, inheritance. Reversed: Suspense, delay, opposition.

Three of Pentacles

A sculptor at his work in a monastery. Compare the design which illustrates the Eight of Pentacles. The apprentice or amateur therein has received his reward and is now at work in earnest. Divinatory Meanings: Metier, trade, skilled labour; usually, however, regarded as a card of nobility, aristocracy, renown, glory. Reversed: Mediocrity, in work and otherwise, puerility, pettiness, weakness.

Two of Pentacles

A young man, in the act of dancing, has a pentacle in either hand, and they are joined by that endless cord which is like the number 8 reversed. Divinatory Meanings: On the one hand it is represented as a card of gaiety, recreation and its connexions, which is the subject of the design; but it is read also as news and messages in writing, as obstacles, agitation, trouble, embroilment. Reversed: Enforced gaiety, simulated enjoyment, literal sense, handwriting, composition, letters of exchange.

Ace of Pentacles

A hand—issuing, as usual, from a cloud—holds up a pentacle. Divinatory Meanings: Perfect contentment, felicity, ecstasy; also speedy intelligence; gold. Reversed: The evil side of wealth, bad intelligence; also great riches. In any case it shews prosperity, comfortable material conditions, but whether these are of advantage to the possessor will depend on whether the card is reversed or not.

The Greater Arcana and their Divinatory Meanings

Such are the intimations of the Lesser Arcana in respect of divinatory art, the veridic nature of which seems to depend on an alternative that it may be serviceable to express briefly. The records of the art are ex hypothesi the records of findings in the past based upon experience; as such, they are a guide to memory, and those who can master the elements may—still ex hypothesi—give interpretations on their basis. It is an official and automatic working. On the other hand, those who have gifts of intuition, of second sight, of clairvoyance—call it as we choose and may—will supplement the experience of the past by the findings of their own faculty, and will speak of that which they have seen in the pretexts of the oracles. It remains to give, also briefly, the divinatory significance allocated by the same art to the Trumps Major.

1. THE MAGICIAN.—Skill, diplomacy, address, subtlety; sickness, pain, loss, disaster, snares of enemies; self-confidence, will; the Querent, if male. Reversed: Physician, Magus, mental disease, disgrace, disquiet.

2. THE HIGH PRIESTESS.—Secrets, mystery, the future as yet unrevealed; the woman who interests the Querent, if male; the Querent herself, if female; silence, tenacity; mystery, wisdom, science. Reversed: Passion, moral or physical ardour, conceit, surface knowledge.

3. THE EMPRESS.—Fruitfulness, action, initiative, length of days; the unknown, clandestine; also difficulty, doubt, ignorance. Reversed: Light, truth, the

unravelling of involved matters, public rejoicings; according to another reading, vacillation.

4. THE EMPEROR.—Stability, power, protection, realization; a great person; aid, reason, conviction; also authority and will. Reversed: Benevolence, compassion, credit; also confusion to enemies, obstruction, immaturity.

5. THE HIEROPHANT.—Marriage, alliance, captivity, servitude; by another account, mercy and goodness; inspiration; the man to whom the Querent has recourse. Reversed: Society, good understanding, concord, overkindness, weakness.

6. THE LOVERS.—Attraction, love, beauty, trials overcome. Reversed: Failure, foolish designs. Another account speaks of marriage frustrated and contrarieties of all kinds.

7. THE CHARIOT.—Succour, providence also war, triumph, presumption, vengeance, trouble. Reversed: Riot, quarrel, dispute, litigation, defeat.

8. FORTITUDE.—Power, energy, action, courage, magnanimity; also complete success and honours. Reversed: Despotism, abuse if power, weakness, discord, sometimes even disgrace.

9. THE HERMIT.—Prudence, circumspection; also and especially treason, dissimulation, roguery, corruption. Reversed: Concealment, disguise, policy, fear, unreasoned caution.

10. WHEEL OF FORTUNE.-Destiny, fortune, success, elevation, luck, felicity. Reversed: Increase, abundance, superfluity.

11. JUSTICE.—Equity, rightness, probity, executive; triumph of the deserving side in law. Reversed: Law in all its departments, legal complications, bigotry, bias, excessive severity.

12. THE HANGED MAN.—Wisdom, circumspection, discernment, trials, sacrifice, intuition, divination, prophecy. Reversed: Selfishness, the crowd, body politic.

13. DEATH.—End, mortality, destruction, corruption also, for a man, the loss of a benefactor for a woman, many contrarieties; for a maid, failure of marriage projects. Reversed: Inertia, sleep, lethargy, petrifaction, somnambulism; hope destroyed.

14. TEMPERANCE.—Economy, moderation, frugality, management, accommodation. Reversed: Things connected with churches, religions, sects, the priesthood, sometimes even the priest who will marry the Querent; also disunion, unfortunate combinations, competing interests.

15. THE DEVIL.—Ravage, violence, vehemence, extraordinary efforts, force, fatality; that which is predestined but is not for this reason evil. Reversed: Evil fatality, weakness, pettiness, blindness.

16. THE TOWER.—Misery, distress, indigence, adversity, calamity, disgrace, deception, ruin. It is a card in particular of unforeseen catastrophe. Reversed:

According to one account, the same in a lesser degree also oppression, imprisonment, tyranny.

17. THE STAR.—Loss, theft, privation, abandonment; another reading says-hope and bright prospects, Reversed: Arrogance, haughtiness, impotence.

18. THE MOON.—Hidden enemies, danger, calumny, darkness, terror, deception, occult forces, error. Reversed: Instability, inconstancy, silence, lesser degrees of deception and error.

19. THE SUN.—Material happiness, fortunate marriage, contentment. Reversed: The same in a lesser sense.

20. THE LAST JUDGMENT.—Change of position, renewal, outcome. Another account specifies total loss though lawsuit. Reversed: Weakness, pusillanimity, simplicity; also deliberation, decision, sentence.

ZERO. THE FOOL.—Folly, mania, extravagance, intoxication, delirium, frenzy, bewrayment. Reversed: Negligence, absence, distribution, carelessness, apathy, nullity, vanity.

21. THE WORLD.—Assured success, recompense, voyage, route, emigration, flight, change of place. Reversed: Inertia, fixity, stagnation, permanence.

It will be seen that, except where there is an irresistible suggestion conveyed by the surface meaning, that which is extracted from the Trumps Major by the divinatory art is at once artificial and arbitrary, as it seems to me, in the highest degree. But of one order are the mysteries of light and of another are those of fantasy. The allocation of a fortune-telling aspect to these cards is the story of a prolonged impertinence.

Some additional Meanings of the Lesser Arcana

WANDS.

King.—Generally favourable may signify a good marriage. Reversed: Advice that should be followed.

Queen.—A good harvest, which may be taken in several senses. Reversed: Goodwill towards the Querent, but without the opportunity to exercise it.

Knight.—A bad card; according to some readings, alienation. Reversed: For a woman, marriage, but probably frustrated.

Page.—Young man of family in search of young lady. Reversed: Bad news.

Ten.—Difficulties and contradictions, if near a good card.

Nine.—Generally speaking, a bad card.

Eight.—Domestic disputes for a married person.

Seven.—A dark child.

Six.—Servants may lose the confidence of their masters; a young lady may be betrayed by a friend. Reversed: Fulfilment of deferred hope.

Five.—Success in financial speculation. Reversed: Quarrels may be turned to advantage.

Four.—Unexpected good fortune. Reversed: A married woman will have beautiful children.

Three.—A very good card; collaboration will favour enterprise.

Two.—A young lady may expect trivial disappointments.

Ace.—Calamities of all kinds. Reversed: A sign of birth.

CUPS.

King.—Beware of ill-will on the part of a man of position, and of hypocrisy pretending to help. Reversed: Loss.

Queen.—Sometimes denotes a woman of equivocal character. Reversed: A rich marriage for a man and a distinguished one for a woman.

Knight.—A visit from a friend, who will bring unexpected money to the Querent. Reversed: Irregularity.

Page.—Good augury; also a young man who is unfortunate in love. Reversed: Obstacles of all kinds.

Ten.—For a male Querent, a good marriage and one beyond his expectations. Reversed: Sorrow; also a serious quarrel.

Nine.—Of good augury for military men. Reversed: Good business.

Eight.—Marriage with a fair woman. Reversed: Perfect satisfaction.

Seven.—Fair child; idea, design, resolve, movement. Reversed: Success, if accompanied by the Three of Cups.

Six.—Pleasant memories. Reversed: Inheritance to fall in quickly.

Five.—Generally favourable; a happy marriage; also patrimony, legacies, gifts, success in enterprise. Reversed: Return of some relative who has not been seen for long.

Four.—Contrarieties. Reversed: Presentiment.

Three.—Unexpected advancement for a military man. Reversed: Consolation, cure, end of the business.

Two.—Favourable in things of pleasure and business, as well as love; also wealth and honour. Reversed: Passion.

Ace.—Inflexible will, unalterable law. Reversed: Unexpected change of position.

SWORDS.

King.—A lawyer, senator, doctor. Reversed: A bad man; also a caution to put an end to a ruinous lawsuit.

Queen.—A widow. Reversed: A bad woman, with ill-will towards the Querent.

Knight.—A soldier, man of arms, satellite, stipendiary; heroic action predicted for soldier. Reversed: Dispute with an imbecile person; for a woman, struggle with a rival, who will be conquered.

Page.—An indiscreet person will pry into the Querent's secrets. Reversed: Astonishing news.

Ten.—Followed by Ace and King, imprisonment; for girl or wife, treason on the part of friends. Reversed: Victory and consequent fortune for a soldier in war.

Nine.—An ecclesiastic, a priest; generally, a card of bad omen. Reversed: Good ground for suspicion against a doubtful person.

Eight.—For a woman, scandal spread in her respect. Reversed: Departure of a relative.

Seven.—Dark girl; a good card; it promises a country life after a competence has been secured. Reversed: Good advice, probably neglected.

Six.—The voyage will be pleasant. Reversed: Unfavourable issue of lawsuit.

Five.—An attack on the fortune of the Querent. Reversed: A sign of sorrow and mourning.

Four.—A bad card, but if reversed a qualified success may be expected by wise administration of affairs. Reversed: A certain success following wise administration.

Three.—For a woman, the flight of her lover. Reversed: A meeting with one whom the Querent has compromised; also a nun.

Two.—Gifts for a lady, influential protection for a man in search of help. Reversed: Dealings with rogues.

Ace.—Great prosperity or great misery. Reversed: Marriage broken off, for a woman, through her own imprudence.

PENTACLES.

King.—A rather dark man, a merchant, master, professor. Reversed: An old and vicious man.

Queen.—Dark woman; presents from a rich relative; rich and happy marriage for a young man. Reversed: An illness.

Knight.—An useful man; useful discoveries. Reversed: A brave man out of employment.

Page.—A dark youth; a young officer or soldier; a child. Reversed: Sometimes degradation and sometimes pillage.

Ten.—Represents house or dwelling, and derives its value from other cards. Reversed: An occasion which may be fortunate or otherwise.

Nine.—Prompt fulfilment of what is presaged by neighbouring cards. Reversed: Vain hopes.

Eight.—A young man in business who has relations with the Querent; a dark girl. Reversed: The Querent will be compromised in a matter of money-lending.

Seven.—Improved position for a lady's future husband. Reversed: Impatience, apprehension, suspicion.

Six.—The present must not be relied on. Reversed: A check on the Querent's ambition.

Five.—Conquest of fortune by reason. Reversed: Troubles in love.

Four.—For a bachelor, pleasant news from a lady. Reversed: Observation, hindrances.

Three.—If for a man, celebrity for his eldest son. Reversed: Depends on neighbouring cards.

Two.—Troubles are more imaginary than real. Reversed: Bad omen, ignorance, injustice.

Ace.—The most favourable of all cards. Reversed: A share in the finding of treasure.

It will be observed (1) that these additamenta have little connexion with the pictorial designs of the cards to which they refer, as these correspond with the more important speculative values; (2) and further that the additional meanings are very often in disagreement with those previously given. All meanings are largely independent of one another and all are reduced, accentuated or subject to modification and sometimes almost reversal by their place in a sequence. There is scarcely any canon of criticism in matters of this kind. I suppose that in proportion as any system descends from generalities to details it becomes naturally the more precarious; and in the records of professional fortune-telling, it offers more of the dregs and lees of the subject. At the same time, divinations based on intuition and second sight are of little practical value unless they come down from the region of universals to that of particulars; but in proportion as this gift is present in a particular case, the specific meanings recorded by past cartomancists will be disregarded in favour of the personal appreciation of card values.

This has been intimated already. It seems necessary to add the following speculative readings.

The Recurrence of Cards in Dealing

In the Natural Position

4 Kings = great honour; 3 Kings = consultation; 2 Kings = minor counsel.

4 Queens = great debate; 3 Queens = deception by women; 2 Queens = sincere friends.

4 Knights = serious matters; 3 Knights = lively debate; 2 Knights = intimacy.

4 Pages = dangerous illness; 3 Pages = dispute; 2 Pages = disquiet.

4 Tens = condemnation; 3 Tens = new condition; 2 Tens = change.

4 Nines = a good friend; 3 Nines = success; 2 Nines = receipt.

4 Eights = reverse; 3 Eights = marriage 2 Eights = new knowledge.

4 Sevens = intrigue; 3 Sevens = infirmity; 2 Sevens = news.

4 Sixes = abundance; 3 Sixes = success; 2 Sixes = irritability.

4 Fives = regularity; 3 Fives = determination; 2 Fives = vigils.

4 Fours = journey near at hand; 3 Fours = a subject of reflection; 2 Fours = insomnia.

4 Threes = progress; 3 Threes = unity 2 Threes = calm.

4 Twos = contention; 3 Twos = security; 2 Twos = accord.

4 Aces = favourable chance; 3 Aces = small success; 2 Aces = trickery.

Reversed

4 Kings = celerity; 3 Kings = commerce 2 Kings = projects.

4 Queens = bad company; 3 Queens = gluttony; 2 Queens = work.

4 Knights = alliance 3 Knights = a duel, or personal encounter; 2 Knights = susceptibility.

4 Pages = privation 3 Pages = idleness 2 Pages = society.

4 Tens = event, happening; 3 Tens disappointment; 2 Tens = expectation justified.

4 Nines = usury; 3 Nines imprudence; 2 Nines = a small profit.

4 Eights = error; 3 Eights a spectacle; 2 Eights = misfortune.

4 Sevens = quarrellers; 3 Sevens = joy; 2 Sevens = women of no repute.

4 Sixes = care; 3 Sixes = satisfaction 2 Sixes = downfall.

4 Fives = order; 3 Fives = hesitation; 2 Fives = reverse.

4 Fours = walks abroad; 3 Fours = disquiet; 2 Fours = dispute.

4 Threes = great success; 3 Threes = serenity; 2 Threes = safety.

4 Twos = reconciliation; 3 Twos apprehension; 2 Twos = mistrust.

4 Aces = dishonour; 3 Aces debauchery; 2 Aces = enemies.

The Art of Tarot Divination

We come now to the final and practical part of this division of our subject, being the way to consult and obtain oracles by means of Tarot cards. The modes of operation are rather numerous, and some of them are exceedingly involved. I set aside those last mentioned, because persons who are versed in such questions believe that the way of simplicity is the way of truth. I set aside also the operations which have been republished recently in that section of The Tarot of the Bohemians which is entitled "The Divining Tarot"; it may be recommended at its proper value to readers who wish to go further than the limits of this handbook. I offer in the first place a short process which has been used privately for many years past in England, Scotland and Ireland. I do not think that it has been published—certainly not in connexion with Tarot cards; I believe that it will serve all purposes, but I will add by way of variation-in the second place what used to be known in France as the Oracles of Julia Orsini.

An Ancient Celtic Method of Divination

This mode of divination is the most suitable for obtaining an answer to a definite question. The Diviner first selects a card to represent the person or, matter about which inquiry is made. This card is called the Significator. Should he wish to ascertain something in connexion with himself he takes the one which corresponds to his personal description. A Knight should be chosen as the Significator if the subject of inquiry is a man of forty years old and upward; a King should be chosen for any male who is under that age a Queen for a woman who is over forty years and a Page for any female of less age.

The four Court Cards in Wands represent very fair people, with yellow or auburn hair, fair complexion and blue eyes. The Court Cards in Cups signify people with light brown or dull fair hair and grey or blue eyes. Those in Swords stand for people having hazel or grey eyes, dark brown hair and dull complexion. Lastly, the Court Cards in Pentacles are referred to persons with very dark brown or black hair, dark eyes and sallow or swarthy complexions. These allocations are subject, however, to the following reserve, which will prevent them being taken too conventionally. You can be guided on occasion by the known temperament of a person; one who is exceedingly dark may be very energetic, and would be better represented by a Sword card than a Pentacle. On the other hand, a very fair subject who is indolent and lethargic should be referred to Cups rather than to Wands.

If it is more convenient for the purpose of a divination to take as the Significator the matter about which inquiry is to be made, that Trump or small card should be selected which has a meaning corresponding to the matter. Let it be supposed that the question is: Will a lawsuit be necessary? In this case, take the Trump No. 11, or justice, as the Significator. This has reference to legal affairs. But if the question is: Shall I be successful in my lawsuit? one of the Court Cards must be chosen as the Significator. Subsequently, consecutive divinations may be performed to ascertain the course of the process itself and its result to each of the parties concerned.

Having selected the Significator, place it on the table, face upwards. Then shuffle and cut the rest of the pack three times, keeping the faces of the cards downwards.

Turn up the top or FIRST CARD of the pack; cover the Significator with it, and say: This covers him. This card gives the influence which is affecting the person or matter of inquiry generally, the atmosphere of it in which the other currents work.

Turn up the SECOND CARD and lay it across the FIRST, saying: This crosses him. It shews the nature of the obstacles in the matter. If it is a favourable card, the opposing forces will not be serious, or it may indicate that something good in itself will not be productive of good in the particular connexion.

Turn up the THIRD CARD; place it above the Significator, and say: This crowns him. It represents (a) the Querent's aim or ideal in the matter; (b) the best that can be achieved under the circumstances, but that which has not yet been made actual.

Turn up the FOURTH CARD; place it below the Significator, and say: This is beneath him. It shews the foundation or basis of the matter, that which has already passed into actuality and which the Significator has made his own.

Turn up the FIFTH CARD; place it on the side of the Significator from which he is looking, and say: This is behind him. It gives the influence that is just passed, or is now passing away.

N.B.—If the Significator is a Trump or any small card that cannot be said to face either way, the Diviner must decide before beginning the operation which side he will take it as facing.

Turn up the SIXTH CARD; place it on the side that the Significator is facing, and say: This is before him. It shews the influence that is coming into action and will operate in the near future.

The cards are now disposed in the form of a cross, the Significator—covered by the First Card—being in the centre.

The next four cards are turned up in succession and placed one above the other in a line, on the right hand side of the cross.

The first of these, or the SEVENTH CARD of the operation, signifies himself—that is, the Significator—whether person or thing-and shews its position or attitude in the circumstances.

The EIGHTH CARD signifies his house, that is, his environment and the tendencies at work therein which have an effect on the matter—for instance, his position in life, the influence of immediate friends, and so forth.

The NINTH CARD gives his hopes or fears in the matter.

The TENTH is what will come, the final result, the culmination which is brought about by the influences shewn by the other cards that have been turned up in the divination.

It is on this card that the Diviner should especially concentrate his intuitive faculties and his memory in respect of the official divinatory meanings attached thereto. It should embody whatsoever you may have divined from the other cards on the table, including the Significator itself and concerning him or it, not excepting such lights upon higher significance as might fall like sparks from heaven if the card which serves for the oracle, the card for reading, should happen to be a Trump Major.

The operation is now completed; but should it happen that the last card is of a dubious nature, from which no final decision can be drawn, or which does not appear to indicate the ultimate conclusion of the affair, it may be well to repeat the operation, taking in this case the Tenth Card as the Significator, instead of the one previously used. The pack must be again shuffled and cut three times and the first ten cards laid out as before. By this a more detailed account of "What will come" may be obtained.

If in any divination the Tenth Card should be a Court Card, it shews that the subject of the divination falls ultimately into the hands of a person represented by that card, and its end depends mainly on him. In this event also it is useful to take the Court Card in question as the Significator in a fresh operation, and discover what is the nature of his influence in the matter and to what issue he will bring it.

Great facility may be obtained by this method in a comparatively short time, allowance being always made for the gifts of the operator-that is to say, his faculty of insight, latent or developed-and it has the special advantage of being free from all complications.

I here append a diagram [list] of the cards as laid out in this mode of divination. The Significator is here facing to the left.

The Significator.
1. That covers him
2. What crosses him.
3. What crowns him.
4. What is beneath him.
5. What is behind him.
6. What is before him.
7. Himself.
8. His house.
9. His hopes or fears.
10. What will come.

An Alternative Method of Reading the Tarot Cards

Shuffle the entire pack and turn some of the cards round, so as to invert their tops.

Let them be cut by the Querent with his left hand.

Deal out the first forty-two cards in six packets of seven cards each, face upwards, so that the first seven cards form the first packet, the following seven the second, and so on-as in the following diagram:—

<7> <7> <7> <7> <7> <7>

Take up the first packet; lay out the cards on the table in a row, from right to left; place the cards of the second packet upon them and then the packets which remain. You will thus have seven new packets of six cards each, arranged as follows—

<6> <6> <6> <6> <6> <6> <6>

Take the top card of each packet, shuffle them and lay out from right to left, making a line of seven cards.

Then take up the two next cards from each packet, shuffle and lay them out in two lines under the first line.

Take up the remaining twenty-one cards of the packets, shuffle and lay them out in three lines below the others.

You will thus have six horizontal lines of seven cards each, arranged after the following manner.

◇ ◇ ◇ ◇ ◇ ◇ ◇
◇ ◇ ◇ ◇ ◇ ◇ ◇
◇ ◇ ◇ ◇ ◇ ◇ ◇
◇ ◇ ◇ ◇ ◇ ◇ ◇
◇ ◇ ◇ ◇ ◇ ◇ ◇

◇◇◇◇◇◇◇

In this method, the Querent—if of the male sex—is represented by the Magician, and if female by the High Priestess; but the card, in either case, is not taken from the pack until the forty-two cards have been laid out, as above directed. If the required card is not found among those placed upon the table, it must be sought among the remaining thirty-six cards, which have not been dealt, and should be placed a little distance to the right of the first horizontal line. On the other hand, if it is among them, it is also taken out, placed as stated, and a card is drawn haphazard from the thirty-six cards undealt to fill the vacant position, so that there are still forty-two cards laid out on the table.

The cards are then read in succession, from right to left throughout, beginning at card No. 1 of the top line, the last to be read being that on the extreme left, or No. 7, of the bottom line.

This method is recommended when no definite question is asked-that is, when the Querent wishes to learn generally concerning the course of his life and destiny. If he wishes to know what may befall within a certain time, this time should be clearly specified before the cards are shuffled.

With further reference to the reading, it should be remembered that the cards must be interpreted relatively to the subject, which means that all official and conventional meanings of the cards may and should be adapted to harmonize with the conditions of this particular case in question—the position, time of life and sex of the Querent, or person for whom the consultation is made.

Thus, the Fool may indicate the whole range of mental phases between mere excitement and madness, but the particular phase in each divination must be judged by considering the general trend of the cards, and in this naturally the intuitive faculty plays an important part.

It is well, at the beginning of a reading, to run through the cards quickly, so that the mind may receive a general impression of the subject-the trend of the destiny—and afterwards to start again—reading them one by one and interpreting in detail.

It should be remembered that the Trumps represent more powerful and compelling forces—by the Tarot hypothesis—than are referable to the small cards.

The value of intuitive and clairvoyant faculties is of course assumed in divination. Where these are naturally present or have been developed by the Diviner, the fortuitous arrangement of cards forms a link between his mind and the atmosphere of the subject of divination, and then the rest is simple. Where intuition fails, or is absent, concentration, intellectual observation and deduction must be used to the fullest extent to obtain a satisfactory result. But intuition, even if apparently dormant, may be cultivated by practice in these divinatory processes. If in doubt as to the exact meaning of a card in a particular connexion, the Diviner is recommended, by those who are versed in the matter, to place his hand on it, try to refrain from thinking of what it ought to be, and note the impressions that arise in his mind. At the beginning this will probably resolve itself into mere guessing and may prove incorrect, but it becomes possible with practice to distinguish between a guess of the conscious mind and an impression arising from the mind which is sub-conscious.

It is not within my province to offer either theoretical or practical suggestions on this subject, in which I have no part, but the following additamenta have been contributed by one who has more titles to speak than all the cartomancists of Europe, if they could shuffle with a single pair of hands and divine with one tongue.

NOTES ON THE PRACTICE OF DIVINATION

1. Before beginning the operation, formulate your question definitely, and repeat it aloud.

2. Make your mind as blank as possible while shuffling the cards.

3. Put out of the mind personal bias and preconceived ideas as far as possible, or your judgment will be tinctured thereby.

4. On this account it is more easy to divine correctly for a stranger than for yourself or a friend.

The Method of Reading by Means of Thirty-five Cards

When the reading is over, according to the scheme set forth in the last method, it may happen-as in the previous case-that something remains doubtful, or it may be desired to carry the question further, which is done as follows:—

Take up the undealt cards which remain over, not having been used in the first operation with 42 cards. The latter are set aside in a heap, with the Querent, face upwards, on the top. The thirty-five cards, being shuffled and cut as before, are divided by dealing into six packets thus:—

Packet I consists of the first SEVEN CARDS

Packet II consists of the SIX CARDS next following in order; Packet III consists of the FIVE CARDS following; Packet IV contains the next FOUR CARDS; Packet V contains Two CARDS; and Packet VI contains the last ELEVEN CARDS. The arrangement will then be as follows:—

<11> <2> <4> <5> <6> <7>

Take up these packets successively; deal out the cards which they contain in six lines, which will be necessarily of unequal length.

THE FIRST LINE stands for the house, the environment and so forth.

THE SECOND LINE stands for the person or subject of the divination.

THE THIRD LINE stands for what is passing outside, events, persons, etc.

THE FOURTH LINE stands for a surprise, the unexpected, etc.

THE FIFTH LINE stands for consolation, and may moderate all that is unfavourable in the preceding lines.

THE SIXTH LINE is that which must be consulted to elucidate the enigmatic oracles of the others; apart from them it has no importance.

These cards should all be read from left to right, beginning with the uppermost line.

It should be stated in conclusion as to this divinatory part that there is no method of interpreting Tarot cards which is not applicable to ordinary playing-cards, but the additional court cards, and above all the Trumps Major, are held to increase the elements and values of the oracles.

And now in conclusion as to the whole matter, I have left for these last words—as if by way of epilogue—one further and final point. It is the sense in which I regard the Trumps Major as containing Secret Doctrine. I do not here mean that I am acquainted with orders and fraternities in which such doctrine reposes and is there found to be part of higher Tarot knowledge. I do not mean that such doctrine, being so preserved and transmitted, can be constructed as imbedded independently in the Trumps Major. I do not mean that it is something apart from the Tarot. Associations exist which have special knowledge of both kinds; some of it is deduced from the Tarot and some of it is apart therefrom; in either case, it is the same in the root-matter. But there are also things in reserve which are not in orders or societies, but are transmitted after another manner. Apart from all inheritance of this kind, let any one who is a mystic consider separately and in combination the Magician, the Fool, the High Priestess, the Hierophant, the Empress, the Emperor, the Hanged Man and the Tower. Let him then consider the card called the Last Judgment. They contain the legend of the soul. The other Trumps Major are the details and—as one might say—the accidents. Perhaps such a person will begin to understand what lies far behind these symbols, by whomsoever first invented and however preserved. If he does, he will see also why I have concerned myself with the subject, even at the risk of writing about divination by cards.

Part 4
Bibliography

A CONCISE BIBLIOGRAPHY OF THE CHIEF WORKS DEALING WITH THE TAROT AND ITS CONNEXIONS

As in spite of its modest pretensions, this monograph is, so far as I am aware, the first attempt to provide in English a complete synoptic account of the Tarot, with its archaeological position defined, its available symbolism developed, and—as a matter of curiosity in occultism—with its divinatory meanings and modes of operation sufficiently exhibited, it is my wish, from the literate standpoint, to enumerate those text-books of the subject, and the most important incidental references thereto, which have come under my notice. The bibliographical particulars that follow lay no claim to completeness, as I have cited nothing that I have not seen with my own eyes; but I can understand that most of my readers will be surprised at the extent of the literature—if I may so term it conventionally—which has grown up in the course of the last 120 years. Those who desire to pursue their inquiries further will find ample materials herein, though it is not a course which I am seeking to commend especially, as I deem that enough has been said upon the Tarot in this place to stand for all that has preceded it. The bibliography itself is representative after a similar manner. I should add that there is a considerable catalogue of cards and works on card-playing in the British Museum, but I have not had occasion to consult it to any extent for the purposes of the present list.

I

Monde Primitf, analyse et compare avec le Monde Moderne. Par M. Court de Gebelin. Vol. 8, 40, Paris, 1781.

The articles on the Jeu des Tarots will be found at pp. 365 to 410. The plates at the end shew the Trumps Major and the Aces of each suit. These are valuable, as indications of the cards at the close of the eighteenth century. They were presumably then in circulation in the South of France, as it is said that at the period in question they were practically unknown at Paris. I have dealt with the claims of the papers in the body of the present work. Their speculations were tolerable enough for their mazy period; but that they are suffered still, and accepted indeed without question, by French occult writers is the most convincing testimony that one can need to the qualifications of the latter for dealing with any question of historical research.

II

The Works of Etteilla. Les Septs Nuances de l'oeuvre philosophique Hermitique; Maniere de se recreer avec le Jeu de Cartes, nommees Tarots; Fragments sur les Hautes Sciences; Philosophie des Hautes Sciences; Jeu des Tarots, ou le Livre de Thoth; Lecons Theoriques et Pratiques du Livre de Thoth—all published between 1783 and 1787.

These are exceedingly rare and were frankly among the works of colportage of their particular period. They contain the most curious fragments on matters within and without the main issue, lucubrations on genii, magic, astrology, talismans, dreams, etc. I have spoken sufficiently in the text of the author's views on the Tarot and his place in its modern history. He regarded it as a work of speaking hieroglyphics, but to translate it was not easy. He, however, accomplished the task that is to say, in his own opinion.

III

An Inquiry into the Antient Greek Game, supposed to have been invented by Palamedes. [By James Christie.] London: 40, 1801.

I mention this collection of curious dissertations because it has been cited by writers on the Tarot. It seeks to establish a close connexion between early games of antiquity and modern chess. It is suggested that the invention attributed to Palamedes, prior to the Siege of Troy, was known in China from a more remote period of antiquity. The work has no reference to cards of any kind whatsoever.

IV

Researches into the History of Playing Cards. By Samuel Weller Singer. 40, London, 1816.

The Tarot is probably of Eastern origin and high antiquity, but the rest of Court de Gebelin's theory is vague and unfounded. Cards were known in Europe prior to the appearance of the Egyptians. The work has a good deal of curious information and the appendices are valuable, but the Tarot occupies comparatively little of the text and the period is too early for a tangible criticism of its claims. There are excellent reproductions of early specimen designs. Those of Court de Gebelin are also given in extenso.

V

Facts and Speculations on Playing Cards. By W. A. Chatto. 8vo, London, 1848.

The author suggested that the Trumps Major and the numeral cards were once separate, but were afterwards combined. The oldest specimens of Tarot cards are not later than 1440. But the claims and value of the volume have been sufficiently described in the text.

VI

Les Cartes a Jouer el la Cartomancie. Par D. R. P. Boiteau d'Ambly. 40, Paris, 1854.

There are some interesting illustrations of early Tarot cards, Which are said to be of Oriental origin; but they are not referred to Egypt. The early gipsy connexion is affirmed, but there is no evidence produced. The cards came with the gipsies from India, where they were designed to shew forth the intentions of "the unknown divinity" rather than to be the servants of profane amusement.

VII

Dogme el Rituel de la Haute Magie. Par Eliphas Levi, 2 vols., demy 8vo, Paris, 1854.

This is the first publication of Alphonse Louis Constant on occult philosophy, and it is also his magnum opus. It is constructed in both volumes on the major Keys of the Tarot and has been therefore understood as a kind of development of their implicits, in the way that these were presented to the mind of the author. To supplement what has been said of this work in the text of the present monograph, I need only add that the section on transmutations in the second volume contains what is termed the Key of Thoth. The inner circle depicts a triple Tau, with a hexagram where the bases join, and beneath is the Ace of Cups. Within the external circle are the letters TARO, and about this figure as a whole are grouped the symbols of the Four Living Creatures, the Ace of Wands, Ace of Swords, the letter Shin, and a magician's candle, which is identical, according to Levi, with the lights used in the Goetic Circle of Black Evocations and Pacts. The triple Tau may be taken to represent the Ace of Pentacles. The only Tarot card given in the volumes is the Chariot, which is drawn by two sphinxes; the fashion thus set has been followed in later days. Those who interpret the work as a kind of commentary on the Trumps Major are the conventional occult students and those who follow them will have only the pains of fools.

VIII
Les Romes. Par J. A. Vaillant. Demy 8vo, Paris, 1857.

The author tells us how he met with the cards, but the account is in a chapter of anecdotes. The Tarot is the sidereal book of Enoch, modelled on the astral wheel of Athor. There is a description of the Trumps Major, which are evidently regarded as an heirloom, brought by the gipsies from Indo-Tartary. The publication of Levi's Dogme et Rituel must, I think, have impressed Vaillant very much, and although in this, which was the writer's most important work, the anecdote that I have mentioned is practically his only Tarot reference, he seems to have gone much further in a later publication—Clef Magique de la Fiction et du Fait, but I have not been able to see it, nor do I think, from the reports concerning it, that I have sustained a loss.

IX
Histoire de la Magie. Par Eliphas Levi. 8vo, Paris, 1860.

The references to the Tarot are few in this brilliant work, which will be available shortly in English. It gives the 21st Trump Major, commonly called the Universe, or World, under the title of Yinx Pantomorph—a seated figure wearing the crown of Isis. This has been reproduced by Papus in Le Tarot Divinataire. The author explains that the extant Tarot has come down to us through the Jews, but it passed somehow into the hands of the gipsies, who brought it with them when they first entered France in the early part of the fifteenth century. The authority here is Vaillant.

X

La Clef des Grands Mysteres. Par Eliphas Levi. 8vo, Paris, 1861.

The frontispiece to this work represents the absolute Key of the occult sciences, given by William Postel and completed by the writer. It is reproduced in The Tarot of the Bohemians, and in the preface which I have prefixed thereto, as indeed elsewhere, I have explained that Postel never constructed a hieroglyphical key. Eliphas Levi identifies the Tarot as that sacred alphabet which has been variously referred to Enoch, Thoth, Cadmus and Palamedes. It consists of absolute ideas attached to signs and numbers. In respect of the latter, there is an extended commentary on these as far as the number ig, the series being interpreted as the Keys of Occult Theology. The remaining three numerals which complete the Hebrew alphabet are called the Keys of Nature. The Tarot is said to be the original of chess, as it is also of the Royal Game of Goose. This volume contains the author's hypothetical reconstruction of the tenth Trump Major, shewing Egyptian figures on the Wheel of Fortune.

XI

L'Homme Rouge des Tuileyies. Par P. Christian. Fcap. 8vo, Paris, 1863.

The work is exceedingly rare, is much sought and was once highly prized in France; but Dr. Papus has awakened to the fact that it is really of slender value, and the statement might be extended. It is interesting, however, as containing the writer's first reveries on the Tarot. He was a follower and imitator of Levi. In the present work, he provides a commentary on the Trumps

Major and thereafter the designs and meanings of all the Minor Arcana. There are many and curious astrological attributions. The work does not seem to mention the Tarot by name. A later Histoire de la Magie does little more than reproduce and extend the account of the Trumps Major given herein.

XII
The History of Playing Cards. By E. S. Taylor. Cr. 8vo, London, 1865.

This was published posthumously and is practically a translation of Boiteau. It therefore calls for little remark on my part. The opinion is that cards were imported by the gipsies from India. There are also references to the so-called Chinese Tarot, which was mentioned by Court de Gebelin.

XIII
Origine des Caries a Jouer. Par Romain Merlin. 40, Paris, 1869.

There is no basis for the Egyptian origin of the Tarot, except in the imagination of Court de Gebelin. I have mentioned otherwise that the writer disposes, to his personal satisfaction, of the gipsy hypothesis, and he does the same in respect of the imputed connexion with India; he says that cards were known in Europe before communication was opened generally with that world about 1494. But if the gipsies were a Pariah tribe already dwelling in the West, and if the cards were a part of their baggage, there is nothing in this contention. The whole question is essentially one of speculation.

XIV
The Platonist. Vol. II, pp. 126-8. Published at St. Louis, Mo., U.S.A., 1884-5. Royal 4to. This periodical, the suspension of which must have been regretted by

many admirers of an unselfish and laborious effort, contained one anonymous article on the Tarot by a writer with theosophical tendencies, and considerable pretensions to knowledge. It has, however, by its own evidence, strong titles to negligence, and is indeed a ridiculous performance. The word Tarot is the Latin Rota = wheel, transposed. The system was invented at a remote period in India, presumably—for the writer is vague—about B.C. 300. The Fool represents primordial chaos. The Tarot is now used by Rosicrucian adepts, but in spite of the inference that it may have come down to them from their German progenitors in the early seventeenth century, and notwithstanding the source in India, the twenty-two keys were pictured on the walls of Egyptian temples dedicated to the mysteries of initiation. Some of this rubbish is derived from P. Christian, but the following statement is peculiar, I think, to the writer: "It is known to adepts that there should be twenty-two esoteric keys, which would make the total number up to 100." Persons who reach a certain stage of lucidity have only to provide blank pasteboards of the required number and the missing designs will be furnished by superior intelligences. Meanwhile, America is still awaiting the fulfilment of the concluding forecast, that some few will ere long have so far developed in that country "as to be able to read perfectly... in that perfect and divine sybilline work, the Taro." Perhaps the cards which accompany the present volume will give the opportunity and the impulse!

XV

Lo Joch de Naips. Per Joseph Brunet y Bellet. Cr. 8vo, Barcelona, 1886.

With reference to the dream of Egyptian origin, the author quotes E. Garth Wilkison's Manners and Customs of the Egyptians as negative evidence at least that cards were unknown in the old cities of the Delta. The history of the subject is sketched, following the chief authorities, but without reference to exponents of the occult schools. The mainstay throughout is Chatto. There are some interesting particulars about the prohibition of cards in Spain, and the appendices include a few valuable documents, by one of which it appears, as already mentioned, that St. Bernardin of Sienna preached against games in general, and cards in particular, so far back as 1423. There are illustrations of rude Tarots, including a curious example of an Ace of Cups, with a phoenix rising therefrom, and a Queen of Cups, from whose vessel issues a flower.

XVI

The Tarot: Its Occult Signification, Use in FortuneTelling, and Method of Play. By S. L. MacGregor Mathers. Sq. 16mo, London, 1888.

This booklet was designed to accompany a set of Tarot cards, and the current packs of the period were imported from abroad for the purpose. There is no pretence of original research, and the only personal opinion expressed by the writer or calling for notice here states that the Trumps Major are hieroglyphic symbols corresponding to the occult meanings of the Hebrew alphabet. Here the authority is Levi, from whom is also derived the brief symbolism allocated to the twenty-two Keys. The divinatory meanings follow, and then the modes of operation. It is a mere sketch written in a pretentious manner and is negligible in all respects.

XVII

Traite Methodique de Science Occulte. Par Papus. 8vo, Paris, 1891.

The rectified Tarot published by Oswald Wirth after the indications of Eliphas Levi is reproduced in this work, which—it may be mentioned—extends to nearly 1,100 pages. There is a section on the gipsies, considered as the importers of esoteric tradition into Europe by means of the cards. The Tarot is a combination of numbers and ideas, whence its correspondence with the Hebrew alphabet. Unfortunately, the Hebrew citations are rendered almost unintelligible by innumerable typographical errors.

XVIII
Eliphas Levi: Le Livre des Splendeurs. Demy 8vo, Paris, 1894.

A section on the Elements of the Kabalah affirms (a) That the Tarot contains in the several cards of the four suits a fourfold explanation of the numbers 1 to 10; (b) that the symbols which we now have only in the form of cards were at first medals and then afterwards became talismans; (c) that the Tarot is the hieroglyphical book of the Thirty-two Paths of Kabalistic theosophy, and that its summary explanation is in the Sepher Yelzirah; (d) that it is the inspiration of all religious theories and symbols; (e) that its emblems are found on the ancient monuments of Egypt. With the historical value of these pretensions I have dealt in the text.

XIX
Clefs Magiques et Clavicules de Salomon Par Eliphas Levi. Sq. 12mo, Paris, 1895.

The Keys in question are said to have been restored in 1860, in their primitive purity, by means of hieroglyphical signs and numbers, without any admixture of Samaritan or Egyptian images. There are rude designs of the Hebrew letters attributed to the Trumps Major, with meanings—most of which are to be found in other works by the same writer. There are also combinations of the letters which enter into the Divine Name; these combinations are attributed to the court cards of the Lesser Arcana. Certain talismans of spirits are in fine furnished with Tarot attributions; the Ace of Clubs corresponds to the Deus Absconditus, the First Principle. The little book was issued at a high price and as something that should be reserved to adepts, or those on the path of adeptship, but it is really without value—symbolical or otherwise.

XX
Les xxii Lames Hermetiques du Tarot Divinatoire. Par R. Falconnier. Demy 8vo, Paris, 1896.

The word Tarot comes from the Sanskrit and means "fixed star," which in its turn signifies immutable tradition, theosophical synthesis, symbolism of primitive dogma, etc. Graven on golden plates, the designs were used by Hermes Trismegistus and their mysteries were only revealed to the highest grades of the priesthood of Isis. It is unnecessary therefore to say that the Tarot is of Egyptian origin and the work of M. Falconnier has been to reconstruct its primitive form, which he does by reference to the monuments—that is to say, after the fashion of Eliphas Levi, he draws the designs of the Trumps Major in imitation of Egyptian art. This production has been hailed by French occultists as presenting the Tarot in its perfection, but the same has been said of the designs of Oswald Wirth, which are quite unlike and not Egyptian at all. To be frank, these kinds of foolery may be as much as can be expected from the Sanctuary of the Comedie-Francaise, to which the author belongs, and it should be reserved thereto.

XXI

The Magical Ritual of the Sanctum Regnum, interpreted by the Tarot Trumps. Translated from the MSS. of Eliphas Levi and edited by W. Wynn Westcott, M.B. Fcap. 8vo, London, 1896.

It is necessary to say that the interest of this memorial rests rather in the fact of its existence than in its intrinsic importance. There is a kind of informal commentary on the Trumps Major, or rather there are considerations which presumably had arisen therefrom in the mind of the French author. For example, the card called Fortitude is an opportunity for expatiation on will as the secret of strength. The Hanged Man is said to represent the completion of the Great Work. Death suggests a diatribe against Necromancy and Goetia; but such phantoms have no existence in "the Sanctum Regnum" of life. Temperance produces only a few vapid commonplaces, and the Devil, which is blind force, is the occasion for repetition of much that has been said already in the earlier works of Levi. The Tower represents the betrayal of the Great Arcanum, and this it was which caused the sword of Samael to be stretched over the Garden of Delight. Amongst the plates there is a monogram of the Gnosis, which is also that of the Tarot. The editor has thoughtfully appended some information on the Trump Cards taken from the early works of Levi and from the commentaries of P. Christian.

XXII

Comment on devient Alchimiste. Par F. Jolivet de Castellot. Sq. 8vo, Paris, 1897.

Herein is a summary of the Alchemical Tarot, which-with all my respect for innovations and inventions-seems to be high fantasy; but Etteilla had reveries of this kind, and if it should ever be warrantable to produce a Key Major in place of the present Key Minor, it might be worth while to tabulate the analogies of these strange dreams. At the moment it will be sufficient to say that there is given a schedule of the alchemical correspondences to the Trumps Major, by which it appears that the juggler or Magician symbolizes attractive force; the High Priestess is inert matter, than which nothing is more false; the Pope is the Quintessence, which—if he were only acquainted with Shakespeare—might tempt the present successor of St. Peter to repeat that "there are more things in heaven and earth, Horatio." The Devil, on the other hand, is the matter of philosophy at the black stage; the Last judgment is the red stage of the Stone; the Fool is its fermentation; and, in fine, the last card, or the World, is the Alchemical Absolute-the Stone itself. If this should encourage my readers, they may note further that the particulars of various chemical combinations can be developed by means of the Lesser Arcana, if these are laid out for the purpose. Specifically, the King of Wands = Gold the Pages or Knaves represent animal substances the King of Cups = Silver; and so forth.

XXIII

Le Grand Arcane, ou l'occultisme devoile. Par Eliphas Levi. Demy 8vo, Paris, 1898.

After many years and the long experience of all his concerns in occultism, the author at length reduces his message to one formula in this work. I speak, of course, only in respect of the Tarot: he says that the cards of Etteilla produce a kind of hypnotism in the seer or seeress who divines thereby. The folly of the psychic reads in the folly of the querent. Did he counsel honesty, it is suggested that he would lose his clients. I have written severe criticisms on occult arts and sciences, but this is astonishing from one of their past professors and, moreover, I think that the psychic occasionally is a psychic and sees in a manner as such.

XXIV

Le Serpent de la Genese—Livre II; La Clef de la Magie Noire. Par Stanislas de Guaita. 8vo, Paris, 1902.

It is a vast commentary on the second septenary of the Trumps Major. Justice signifies equilibrium and its agent; the Hermit typifies the mysteries of solitude; the Wheel of Fortune is the circulus of becoming or attaining; Fortitude signifies the power resident in will; the Hanged Man is magical bondage, which speaks volumes for the clouded and inverted insight of this fantasiast in occultism: Death is, of course, that which its name signifies, but with reversion to the second death; Temperance means the magic of transformations, and therefore suggests excess rather than abstinence. There is more of the same kind of thing—I believe—in the first book, but this will serve as a specimen. The demise of Stanislas de Guaita put an end to his scheme of interpreting the Tarot Trumps, but it should be understood that the connexion is shadowy and that actual references could be reduced to a very few pages.

XXV

Le Tarot: Apercu historique. Par. J. J. Bourgeat. Sq. 12MO, Paris, 1906.

The author has illustrated his work by purely fantastic designs of certain Trumps Major, as, for example, the Wheel of Fortune, Death and the Devil. They have no connexion with symbolism. The Tarot is said to have originated in India, whence it passed to Egypt. Eliphas Levi, P. Christian, and J. A. Vaillant are cited in support of statements and points of view. The mode of divination adopted is fully and carefully set out.

XXVI

L'Art de tirer les Caries. Par Antonio Magus. Cr. 8vo, Paris, n.d. (about 1908).

This is not a work of any especial pretension, nor has it any title to consideration on account of its modesty. Frankly, it is little—if any—better than a bookseller's experiment. There is a summary account of the chief methods of divination, derived from familiar sources; there is a history of cartomancy in France; and there are indifferent reproductions of Etteilla Tarot cards, with his meanings and the well-known mode of operation. Finally, there is a section on common fortune-telling by a piquet set of ordinary cards: this seems to lack the only merit that it might have Possessed, namely, perspicuity; but I speak with reserve, as I am not perhaps a judge possessing ideal qualifications in matters of this kind. In any case, the question signifies nothing. It is just to add that the concealed author maintains what he terms the Egyptian tradition of the Tarot, which is the Great Book of Thoth. But there is a light accent throughout his thesis, and it does not follow that he took the claim seriously.

XXVII

Le Tarot Divinatoire: Clef du tirage des Caries et des sorts. Par le Dr. Papus. Demy 8vo, Paris, 1909.

The text is accompanied by what is termed a complete reconstitution of all the symbols, which means that in this manner we have yet another Tarot. The Trumps Major follow the traditional lines, with various explanations and attributions on the margins, and this Plan obtains throughout the series. From the draughtsman's point of view, it must be said that the designs are indifferently done, and the reproductions seem worse than the designs. This is probably of no especial importance to the class of readers addressed.

Dr. Papus also presents, by way of curious memorials, the evidential value of which he seems to accept implicitly, certain unpublished designs of Eliphas Levi; they are certainly interesting as examples of the manner in which the great occultist manufactured the archaeology of the Tarot to bear out his personal views. We have (a) Trump Major, No. 5, being Horus as the Grand Hierophant, drawn after the monuments; (b) Trump Major, No. 2, being the High Priestess as Isis, also after the monuments; and (c) five imaginary specimens of an Indian Tarot. This is how la haute science in France contributes to the illustration of that work which Dr. Papus terms livre de la science eternelle; it would be called by rougher names in English criticism. The editor himself takes his usual pains and believes that he has discovered the time attributed to each card by ancient Egypt. He applies it to the purpose of divination, so that the skilful fortune-teller can now predict the hour and the day when the dark young man will meet with the fair widow, and so forth.

XXVIII

Le Tarot des Bohemiens. Par Papus. 8vo, Paris, 1889. English Translation, second edition, 1910.

An exceedingly complex work, which claims to present an absolute key to occult science. It was translated into English by Mr. A. P. Morton in 1896, and this version has been re-issued recently under my own supervision. The preface which I have prefixed thereto contains all that it is necessary to say regarding its claims, and it should be certainly consulted by readers of the present Pictorial Key to the Tarot. The fact that Papus regards the great sheaf of hieroglyphics as "the most ancient book in the world," as "the Bible of Bibles," and therefore as "the primitive revelation," does not detract from the claim of his general study, which—it should be added—is accompanied by numerous valuable plates, exhibiting Tarot codices, old and new, and diagrams summarizing the personal theses of the writer and of some others who preceded him. The Tarot of the Bohemians is published at 6s. by William Rider & Son, Ltd.

XXIX

Manuel Synthetique et Pratique du Tarot. Par Eudes Picard. 8vo, Paris, 1909.

Here is yet one more handbook of the subject, presenting in a series of rough plates a complete sequence of the cards. The Trumps Major are those of Court de Gebelin and for the Lesser Arcana the writer has had recourse to his imagination; it can be said that some of them are curious, a very few thinly suggestive and the rest bad. The explanations embody neither research nor thought at first hand; they are bald summaries of the occult authorities in France, followed by a brief general sense drawn out as a harmony of the whole. The method of use is confined to four pages and recommends that divination should be performed in a fasting state. On the history of the Tarot, M. Picard says (a) that it is confused; (b) that we do not know precisely whence it comes; (c) that, this notwithstanding, its introduction is due to the Gipsies. He says finally that its interpretation is an art.

Manufactured by Amazon.ca
Bolton, ON